CHICANO ROOTS
GO DEEP

CHICANO ROOTS GO DEEP

HAROLD COY

Foreword by
DR. JOSÉ VÁZQUEZ-AMARAL

DODD, MEAD & COMPANY
New York

The Mexican designs are reprinted from *Design Motifs of Ancient Mexico* by Jorge Enciso, Dover Publications, Inc., 1953. Map by Salem Tamer.

Library of Congress Cataloging in Publication Data

Coy, Harold.
    Chicano roots go deep.

    Bibliography: p.
    Includes index.
    SUMMARY: Traces the history of the Chicanos in the
United States and discusses their general and individual
influences on and problems living in an Anglo culture.
    1. Mexican Americans—Juvenile literature.
    [1. Mexican Americans]   I. Title.
 E 184.M5C68   973'.04'6872   75-11434
    ISBN 0-396-07186-4

TO A CHICANO COUPLE
WHO SHARED THEIR HUT
BY A RAILROAD SIDING
WITH A STRANGER
MANY YEARS AGO

FOREWORD

Harold coy's *Chicano Roots Go Deep* is recommended reading for all Americans. All Chicanos should carry a copy, as they do their social security numbers or voters' registration cards, to remind themselves and their Anglo brethren that the Southwest is theirs by right, the right of the first occupant. The Anglos should also own a copy of the book to gain a much-needed insight into the Chicano who is too often looked down upon as an intruder in the Promised Land. This is an admirable book teeming with human facts and figures that tell of the original winning of the West and Southwest by civilizers from Mexico, centuries before the padres and conquistadors came in the sixteenth century.

Ancestors of today's Chicanos have deep roots on this continent. The primitive civilizations of the Navajos and the Pueblos of the U.S. Southwest were pale reflections of the great Middle American cultures that date back thousands of years. Man had been living and hunting the mammoth on the volcanic Mexican highlands in 8000 B.C.; the great

Olmec culture at La Venta flourished around 800 B.C., that is to say, about the time of Homeric Greece. The Olmecs then possessed several scientific principles that came only many centuries later in Europe, among them the invention of the concept of zero and positional numbers (where to put the ones, tens, hundreds, and so on, to make complicated mathematics possible) and astronomical knowledge that made their calendar more precise than the one brought by the Europeans about two thousand years later.

The European ancestors of the Chicanos were the conquering Spaniards, supermen of their century and conquerors of what was truly called the New World. Spain was the center of the political world and financial power; her representatives discovered and explored almost half the globe, circumnavigated the planet to prove that it was round, and fathered a new race: the *mestizo* or Ibero-American.

Chicano Roots Go Deep proves that given the right kind of material and chronicler, history is an absorbing drama whose players are the same people we see going about today's streets. Harold Coy inaugurates a new era in writing about the Chicano or Mexican American minority. It is not easy to be objective and sympathetic at the same time, especially when dealing with a subject thickly overlaid with more than a century's prejudice and feelings of guilt. Coy's contribution to the literature on the Chicano, thoroughly based on scholarly research, is eminently readable. It will surely be used as an indispensable source for any and all later books written on the subject and by extension on other minorities in our "melting pot" where they so frequently refuse to melt. We are indeed fortunate and very much in Harold Coy's debt for having provided us with a distilled outline of one of the missing pieces in that most absorbing and promising human mosaic, the United States of America.

> DR. JOSÉ VÁZQUEZ-AMARAL
> Chairman of the Department
>   of Spanish and Portuguese
> Rutgers University
> New Brunswick, New Jersey

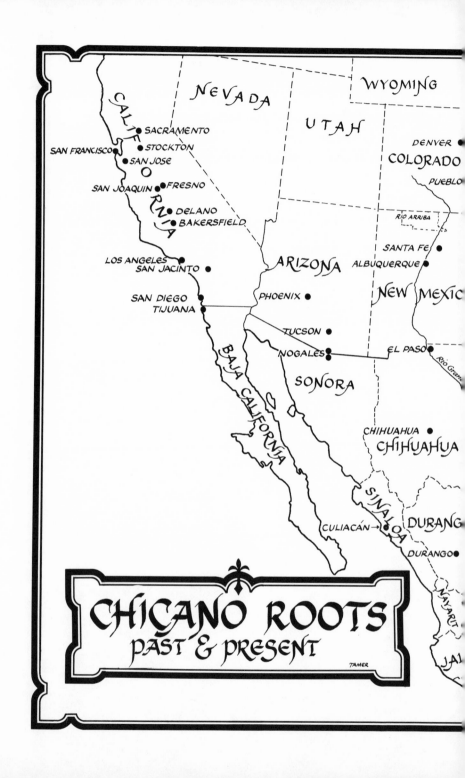

CONTENTS

1
THE
CHANGING
BARRIOS

 CHAPTER 1

A PEOPLE LOOKING FOR A NAME

M R. Garcia was born in Texas like all his family line since the days of the open range. But to his Anglo-American neighbors he's not an American but a Mexican. Some pronounce it "Meskin" and imagine it's more polite to call Mr. Garcia a Latin American or a Latino. He himself never doubted he was a Mexican—that is, until recently, when on an impulse he took a Greyhound bus and rode to Mexico City.

Mr. Garcia told himself he wanted to know his own people better. He has a warm personality and made friends readily but had unexpected communication problems. For example, while crossing a busy street in the Mexican capital with a companion, he cried, *"Wátchele, la troca!"* (Watch it, the truck!) instead of *"¡Cuidado con el camión!"* It's lucky they weren't hit. Mr. Garcia's Mexican friends also were puzzled by words like *aiscrin* (ice cream), *jai escul* (high school),

3

and *los fonis* for *los monos,* the funny papers. In Mexico such
near-English expressions are *pochismos*—and a man using
them may be called a *pocho,* though Mr. Garcia's hosts, being
even politer than his Texas neighbors, did not do so. Still, he
came home aware that he'd been in a foreign land. He was
not Mexican. He was not American. What was he?

This is a question that millions have been asking themselves. West of the Mississippi—and overwhelmingly in the
Southwestern states—people of Mexican descent are the nation's largest minority. In the United States as a whole, only
black Americans outnumber them. In northern New Mexico
many call themselves Spanish Americans or Hispanos; in
Texas, Tejanos or Texas Mexicans; in California, Mexicanos.
A more inclusive name is Mexican-Americans, or Mexican
Americans without the hyphen, which some find objec-
tionable. Others take exception to any special name: "We are
just Americans." Nevertheless, they find themselves looked
upon as a group apart. Formerly, the more light-complexioned sometimes changed their names or called themselves
"Spanish" in order to blend more easily with the majority
group. Few would do so today: it seems like a humiliating
denial of what one is and should take pride in being.

Well, then, if one is neither American nor Mexican, what
is he? In the search for a name, Chicano has come into wide
use since the middle 1960s. It is a form of Mexicano. Drop
the first syllable, start the next one with a *ch* sound, and you
have it. It derives ultimately from the Aztecs, who called
themselves the Mexica (pronounced may-she-kah) and whom

the Spaniards called Mexicanos.

To Spanish-speaking Californians, early in this century, a Chicano was a newly arrived immigrant in the sense of a greenhorn or a country cousin. By the 1920s, West Coast migratory workers were calling one another Chicano without giving or taking offense. But if one settled down in a steady job he might feel that Chicano was not quite dignified, not quite "American" enough. That is how it was until the stirring events of the late 1960s—the great grape strike, the explosive growth of big-city *barrios* (Spanish-speaking neighborhoods), and student activity inspired in part by the Black Power movement—served to heighten the need for a common name. An ethnic vanguard then came forward and claimed the humble term Chicano as a badge of honor. Such things have happened before. Wasn't Yankee a Redcoat's term of derision before New England's rebellious colonists proudly took it for a name?

Not all older persons of Mexican descent liked being called Chicanos, and some still resent it as drawing a line between themselves and other Americans. They disapprove of their sons (and even more, of their daughters!) carrying banners and picket signs. Such conduct seems undignified and likely to lead to trouble, of which they have more than enough already.

The young tend though to favor the term. Many would be nothing else. And their views count, for every other Mexican American is under twenty. "It is a name we have given to ourselves, not one that has been forced upon us," says the writer Armando B. Rendon. Since 1970, "Chicano" has been winning acceptance, even among older people. It is used increasingly in the press, in college course descriptions, even in government publications, and seems to be here to stay, along with "Mexican American" as a more formal alternative.

A collective name for Chicanos is *La Raza*. This doesn't mean "The Race" in the English-language sense. It's more like "Our People" and embraces all who are *carnales,* blood brothers, regardless of complexion, eye color, or texture of hair. "He's *raza,"* one Chicano will say of another, though to an outsider's prejudiced eye they may look as unlike as a Castilian and an Aztec.

CHAPTER 2

THE LAND
OF AZTLÁN

How many Chicanos are there? No one knows exactly. Estimates made in the 1970s ranged from six to eight million—and going up fast. The census-takers lack a definition that includes all Chicanos. Social scientists, by counting Spanish surnames like Alvarez, Aguirre, Baca, Garza, Lopez, Muñoz, Perez, Ruiz, and Treviño, can estimate the ratio of Chicanos to the total population in the Southwestern states. But in the East a Spanish surname may stem from Puerto Rico, Cuba, or elsewhere. There must be over ten million such names in the United States, of which a majority, though not all, belong to Chicanos.

Any count is further complicated by the flow of Mexican nationals, or citizens, across the border. "Green carders," for example, are entitled to work in the United States but may live, as many do, in Mexico. Every day they cross by thousands from border towns into El Paso and the San Diego area. Far more numerous are those without papers, the so-called illegals or wetbacks, whose only crime, as one immigration official put it, is being hungry. Anxious for work and wages in the United States, they are ready to swim the Rio Grande if necessary. Few actually swim. They either wade or cross the desert borderlands west of El Paso. The real obstacle is *la migra,* the Border Patrol of the immigration authorities. The blue-uniformed agents in their Texas hats catch tens or even hundreds of thousands every year and return them to Mexico, but many keep on trying and finally make it to Los Angeles or points north. This situation arouses mixed feelings. When melons lie unpicked in the fields and dishes pile up unwashed in vacation hotels, employers ask few questions of job-seekers, though it's convenient, of course, if they will go away quietly when work is slack. The Chicanos, for their part, are torn between sympathy for their needy blood brothers from the "other side" and the dread of being under-cut in the cheap labor market.

Nearly nine-tenths of all Chicanos are native-born citizens of the United States. But they "look Mexican" and do well to have a birth certificate always with them. Not long ago a young Texas Chicano was picked up in the Florida tomato fields without proof of citizenship. He was speedily flown to the nearest point in Mexico, which happens to be across the entrance of the Gulf of Mexico in Yucatán. Nearest, that is, as the goose flies. Not being a goose, the youth was obliged to return via the long sweeping curve of the Gulf coast. He was two months hitching rides and living on handouts from hospitable Mexicans before he reached the Texas border and could telephone his family to come and identify him.

The typical Chicano used to be, but no longer is, a fruit picker. Old-time Californians remember the picking teams coming into the orange groves with their ladders and equipment: shears for cutting the stem, cotton gloves to protect the fruit from fingernail cuts, and collecting bags that opened in front so that the oranges might be rolled gently into the box, not poured. Today the trees are falling before the power saws to make room for real estate developments. There are machines for picking not only citrus but tomatoes, peas, cotton, and other crops. Four out of five Chicanos have moved to the city—or else the city has moved to them, enveloping the labor camps from which their fathers went out to the fields. Some of the camps have become "doughnut communities," defined as "holes where the poor live surrounded by people with dough." Yesterday's fruit picker is today's hod carrier or car washer.

Many of the barrios where city-dwelling Chicanos live have unromantic names like El Hoyo, The Hole, of which there's one in Los Angeles, another in Tucson. Goat Hill in Denver recalls the efforts of one-time country folk to survive in the city with a goat and a garden. San Antonio's La Tripa is a gutsy name inspired by a neighboring slaughterhouse. Wherever Chicanos are huddled on the margins of a swamp or by the gasworks under a blanket of smog, there's likely to be a Sal Si Puedes. The name means Get Out If You Can. Some get out in trailers and settle along the highways leading from the city. Or they build tin-roofed shacks from discarded lumber, including the containers in which IBM computers were shipped.

In the hot lands, extending from South Texas through Arizona, La Raza builds with sun-dried adobe bricks, a tried and true insulating material. Los Angeles is bungalow land. Tiny Chicano bungalows in pinks and yellows cling to slopes and nestle in ravines. East Los Angeles is Chicano, as are San Antonio's Westside and Phoenix south of Buchanan Street. Directions differ, but the barrios are always on the wrong side of the tracks. They've been called "sunshine slums" and are given over less to grimy tenements than to modest cottages, each with its TV aerial, songbirds, and flowering plants. The Chicanos say, "Where there are flowers and birds, there are women, and where there are women, no one goes hungry."

Chicanos often call their land Aztlán for the legendary homeland of the Aztecs, which lay somewhere northwest of the Valley of Mexico. Today Aztlán, geographically speaking, is the Southwest. An eighth of the surnames in Texas, New Mexico, Colorado, Arizona, and California are Spanish, though the ratio varies with the region. Brownsville, Laredo, and the South Texas Winter Garden are overwhelmingly Chicano in population. San Antonio and Los Angeles are the twin capitals of Aztlán, where many live and work and some pass the winter before leaving for the sugar beet fields of Michigan or starting a circuit that will end in the Idaho potato fields.

El Paso marks the place where the Rio Grande cuts

through a mountain barrier for its southeasterly sweep to the Gulf of Mexico. The city's population is half Chicano and looks even more so because of the workers and shoppers who are there from Ciudad Juárez, across the river in Mexico. El Paso has been the port of entry for millions who have traveled up Mexico's arterial highway No. 45 from the impoverished western hills of the Central Plateau to work and often to stay in the United States.

Up the Rio Grande in New Mexico are places with Spanish names, including Santa Fe, oldest state capital in the United States. In mountain pastures as far north as Colorado, Hispano sheepmen cling to an old, more communal way of life than Anglos know. But they find themselves increasingly hemmed in by dude ranches and national forests. The young people find jobs in Albuquerque's defense plants and return to the home place, if at all, for weekend reunions. It's nice for the children to see *abuelita,* their grandmother, though too bad they can hardly talk with her, what with their city English and her country Spanish.

Denver rates a big circle on the Chicano map as a cultural center, a place of work, and a labor market from which to ship out to the mines and beet fields. Tucson, an old Mexican pueblo in Arizona, is now a thriving city where Chicanos find jobs in the air-conditioning and refrigeration industries. The newer Phoenix has come to rival Southern California in its swift and many-sided growth.

California is the No. 1 Chicano state, long since surpassing even Texas. San Diego, Bakersfield, Fresno, Stockton, and

Sacramento stand out on the map of Aztlán. Large Chicano communities dot the San Francisco Bay area, south to San Jose and beyond. But the world capital of Chicanismo, as no one will doubt, is Los Angeles.

There are said to be more than a million Chicanos in and around Los Angeles. No one is sure, one reason being that here Chicanos and Anglos intermarry more than in other places, much more, certainly, than in Texas. Mr. Jones takes his beautiful Chicana secretary for his bride. Mr. Rodriguez marries a blue-eyed blonde. Someone checked the Spanish surnames on Los Angeles marriage licenses and found one in four marrying a non-Chicano. To which culture will their children belong?

Be that as it may, Los Angeles will be more rather than less Chicano as time goes on. For the Chicano community is constantly replenished with transfusions of new blood. Texas Mexicans are drawn by visions of a new chance in California. Mexicans come from the interior via El Paso. "TJs" cross from Tijuana. Chicanos are living in new barrios and mixed neighborhoods beyond the confines of East Los Angeles and as far away as Long Beach and Pomona. Urban renewal has hastened their spreading out. Four freeways cutting swaths through East Los Angeles have dispersed old neighborhoods and broken up the familiar associations of corner grocery, barber shop, dance hall, and Spanish-language movie house. There's a Chicano saying that urban renewal means Mexican removal. But the result has been to seed new communities. Many say that Los Angeles, or at least its central part, is destined to be a Chicano city.

Chicanos are not wanderers by choice, but the constant inflow of job-seekers from Mexico and the rural Southwest tends to bring down wages. As a result, breadwinners and whole families go north, at first to work in the harvests but later, perhaps, to "settle out" and stay. Thus Chicano colonies have taken root in Washington State, Oregon, Utah, Idaho, Nebraska, Iowa, and Ohio. Some big-city Chicano communities began as long ago as World War I, when laborers were brought in to work on the railroads and in packing houses and steel mills. Kansas City and Milwaukee are cases in point, while the Chicago-Gary area has a huge Chicano population.

Perhaps one Chicano in seven now lives outside the Southwest—the geographical Aztlán. If a Chicano rents a room on Blue Island Avenue in Chicago, has he departed from Aztlán? No, some would say, not if he continues to cherish his Chicano culture. For Aztlán is more than contiguous territory. It is something a Chicano carries in his heart wherever he goes.

 CHAPTER 3

BARRIO HAPPENINGS

A CHICANO without song would be like a duck out of water. The sound of music is his natural element. When he's host at a party, a *fiestecita,* he brings out his guitar, or calls on a talented guest, and everyone sings old Agustín Lara favorites like "Solamente una vez" ("Only Once"), or *rancheras* (country songs of romantic passion and unrequited love), or, just as likely, the current English-language hits.

The guitarist's grandfather could have been a professional troubadour, singing *corridos,* or ballads, in praise of heroes who lived bravely and died nobly. If so, he would have gained his living selling the words on sheets of flimsy pink or green paper. But if his grandson has similar ambitions, he will join a band with a name like Los Enemigos del Sueño (Enemies of Sleep) and will entertain at dances, wedding receptions, baptisms, and saint's day parties. If very successful, he will become a radio singer.

More than a hundred Spanish-language radio and television

stations operate in the United States. KMEX-TV of Los Angeles ties in with other stations in California and Texas and can transform a popular singer into a familiar face and voice all over the Southwest. These broadcasting media support the Chicano in his aspirations, record his triumphs, and reflect his culture. They provide spot news coverage and bring Mexican serials into Chicano homes, along with international *futbol* matches—the game Anglos call soccer.

Women listeners have their favorite commentators. The *Chicano Times* critic, for example, likes Martita on Channel 4 in San Antonio because she sincerely identifies with the barrio poor. She's not one of those *chocantonas,* or highfalutin ladies, who pretend they are so Americanized that they can't pronounce their own names in Spanish. The tuned-in housewife also hears commercials for frozen tortillas, those thin corn cakes that serve as bread or, when rolled up with a meat-and-bean filling, become tacos. The announcer's problem is that many a wife and mother still feels duty bound to make her own tortillas. It is well, he concedes, for the *señora* to be self-sacrificing up to a point, but need she support the drudgery of grinding her own corn when instant *masa,* or tortilla dough, is conveniently packaged by Quaker Oats?

A high percentage of Chicanos hold low-paying jobs in bakeries, hotels and restaurants, filling stations, and the building and clothing trades. Chicano hands may be roughened by toil but their five senses are buffed to a high polish and respond to bright colors, the feel of fabrics, pungent foods, and the sights and sounds coming from where the action is. Barrio artists abound, not only painters and sculptors, but potters, weavers, poets, theater people, and film and video tape makers. For many their art is an *afición,* a hobby, rather than a full-time profession, but cumulatively it enriches the barrios with galleries, shops, studios, and mural paintings inspired by the Chicano present, the Mexican Revolution of 1910, and Mexico's Indian past. Chicano ballet and theater troupes go on tour, and in Lincoln Park, Los Angeles, the Plaza de la Raza is taking shape as a great cultural center.

May 5, the *Cinco de Mayo,* is a holiday in the barrios, marking a memorable battle in 1862 when the Mexicans turned back the French invaders at Puebla and gave Benito Juárez time to organize the stubborn resistance that saved his country's independence. Few Anglos know that it also gave Lincoln time. For had the Mexican line not held in Puebla, the invaders would have advanced to the Texas border and made common cause with the Confederacy in the Civil War.

September 16 is the high point of the Chicano year. It commemorates the *Grito* or cry which Father Miguel Hidalgo raised in 1810 on the steps of his parish church at Dolores, in Guanajuato, sparking Mexico's eleven-year-long struggle for independence from Spain. Festivities begin on the night of the fifteenth, perhaps with a coronation ball, as in Los Angeles, where Miss Barrios Unidos is chosen from among lovely candidates who represent East Los Angeles, Pico Rivera, El Monte, the Harbor Area, and Pomona Valley. Next morning comes the parade, with bands and floats, marching contingents with banners, horsemen in splendid *charro* costumes, and, alongside, vendors crying their tamales and tacos. The destination is an open assembly place like the football stadium. Here thousands gather in their weathered jeans or Sunday best for a stirring ceremony in two languages and a reenactment of the Grito by the Mexican consul or a visiting Mexican dignitary. The cry of "Viva México!" rises from the massed spectators, who then go on from enthusiasm to rhythmic clapping and coyote yells as musical ensembles, top name bands, and famous soloists with Pancho Villa mustaches take their turns before the microphone.

CHAPTER 4

TACOS OR HAMBURGERS?

BEFORE coming to KMEX, Danny Villanueva was a player with the Dallas Cowboys. He's hefty for a Chicano and feels at home both in the Anglos' culture and his own. But this, he recalls, was not always so. His parents had taught him to bow his head as a sign of respect when spoken to by adults. So that's what he'd do when his teacher corrected him. But she, being Anglo and misreading the signal, would sternly command, "Look me in the eye when you are spoken to." Danny was caught between two cultures, as are so many Chicanos.

What are the highest values of Chicano culture? Recently a Chicana women's conference at Texas A & I defined them as *Respeto, Orgullo, Corazón,* and *Idioma* (Respect, Pride, Heart or Feeling, and Language). These values pervade the home and the barrio. Children respect their parents, do assigned chores with no back talk, and show deference to their father. An older brother is also entitled to respect. He is second in command and may some day head the family. Meanwhile, he defends you against the neighborhood bully. Count on his loyalty but don't "horse around" with him.

Pride consists of self-respect and a sense of dignity. In the *palomilla,* a teen-ager learns to hold his own with boys of his age. This is not a street gang, as the police sometimes imagine, but a casual gathering of age mates, testing one another and asserting their right to respect, more by the tongue than the fist.

A man retains his dignity by looking after his family and being *serio, feo, fuerte y formal* (serious, stern, strong, and formal). He never raises his voice to another man unless looking for a fight nor does he shout to attract attention when a friendly whistle and a suitable gesture will serve to pass the time of day or indicate a desire to chat.

A man full of years bears the honorary title of Don, particularly if he has minded his own business and been generous to others. No matter that José Fuentes has a hole in his shirt. He's still Don José. One day, though, poverty drives him to the beet fields. Imagine the humiliation the old man then feels at being called plain Joe.

Feeling or Heart can be a manly virtue. "There's something of the musician, poet, and crazy guy in us all," they say in the barrio (*De músico, poeta y loco, todos tenemos un poco*). But feeling is particularly appropriate in a woman. She lavishes affection on the children, and they possess the emotional security of belonging to a family. The poet Abelardo Delgado suggests that it's not which of various names they

call his people that matters; what counts is what is taken in
with an Indian mother's milk. Chicanitos may enter school
speaking little English and unacquainted with middle-class
lifeways, but their imagination is well developed and, when
asked to make up stories from picture cards, they excel in
creating characters and situations.

Language, in the barrio, means Spanish. José Angel Gu-
tierrez, who has led La Raza to election victories in Crystal
City, Texas, calls Spanish "the soul language of our people."
English is essential for taking part in the larger society, but
Spanish seals the unity of the Chicano people and makes the
culture of their ancestors an open book.

Too many children, unfortunately, are denied a chance to
know either language well. Coming from Spanish-speaking
homes, they enter a first grade of incomprehensible English
speech. Try as they will to understand, they lag behind in
their studies and many eventually drop out, "illiterate in two
languages," as a rueful saying has it. Dropouts and *vatos locos*
(street kids), unschooled in literary Spanish, communicate in
a dialect rich in Spanish slang and their own inventions.
"Ponte trucha, mano" (Wise up, brother), says Nacho (Ignacio)
to Lalo (Eduardo). *Mano* is short for *hermano,* brother. Were
Nacho given to half-English words, he'd say *broda.* Chicano
poets weave street dialect into their works with artistic effect,
but a fellow also needs standard Spanish and English to make
his way in a wider world.

As it is, some Chicanos are more at home in Spanish,
others in English. A Mexican comic strip, picturing Emiliano

Villa

17, R̶i̶ 47

137, 172

Zapata

20, 21, 47

114, 165

Tijerina

146-149

Teacher_____

Class_____

Date_____

1 2 3 4 5 6 7

Teacher _____

Class _____

Date _____

    1   2   3   4   5   6   7

Zapata

pp. 20 -21

p. 47

p. 114

p. 165

p. 170

p. 188

Zapata's revolutionary fight for land and liberty, is a popular feature in Chicano papers, but they translate the Spanish dialogue into English captions so that their readers will understand it in one language or the other.

Even children, counting out players in a game, are caught between cultures. Should they switch to the eenie, meenie, miney, mo routine or stay with *tin, marín, de do pingüe, cúcara, mácara, títere, fué?* In the holiday season, is Santa Claus more important than the Three Holy Kings?

Santa is winning out, even in Mexico, but traditional foods are not forgotten. The Christmas turkey, if any, tastes better if served in a *mole* sauce of chiles, chocolate, and spices. Chile con carne is more Texan than Mexican, but *carnitas* (chunks of pork) are international, like *chicharrones* (crisply fried pieces of pigskin), and bitingly hot *chorizo* sausages. A *barbacoa* is good wherever one can dig a pit, line it with hot stones, and wrap the lamb or *cabrito* (kid or young goat) in maguey (century plant) leaves.

An old-fashioned family, caught between two cultures, has to make adjustments here and there. How can they afford color TV unless *Mamacita* contributes to the income? But if she works all day in a laundry or at a power sewing machine, how can she prepare a quick meal without frozen foods and an electric blender? The children call her *la jefa,* the chief, and she begins to feel "more equal" within the family circle. *Papacito* may be wounded in his *machismo,* which can mean anything from manly courage to male chauvinism. To make matters worse, Lucha, his daughter, is dating boys without his approval.

Thus the Chicano family bends, with some discomfort, to city life and Anglo ways. But it does not break, and its resistance is strengthened by its links within the barrio. If its roots go back two or three generations, there will be scores of cousins whose womenfolk are ready to nurse the sick or help with the housework when a new baby is arriving. Kinship, moreover, is not limited by ties of blood or marriage. When parents choose godparents to sponsor a newborn child in baptism, they and the other couple become *compadres* and are henceforth like brothers and sisters. Compadre ties may weaken in the city, but there are some who believe that a new sense of Chicano solidarity will reinvigorate this time-honored institution.

Ideally, all Chicanos are brothers, *carnales,* preferring cooperation to competition. They have benefit societies for mutual aid in sickness and death, and clubs for buying rice and beans in wholesale lots. They will volunteer for a "paint-in" to brighten the houses of the bedridden and elderly or translate in court for a brother whose English is faulty. Chicanos who have "made it"—teachers, doctors, lawyers, priests—are always serving as middlemen between their tongue-tied neighbors and government officials.

If Mexican Americans were Polish or Swedish, dispersed through the country and far from their homeland, they might gradually lose their identity as a separate group. Mexican Americans, so close to their origins, face a different situation. If they try to change cultures, they find that a bronze skin often bars the way to employment, housing, and social acceptance. The United States Civil Rights Commission reports that their very appearance makes them "suspicious" to those unacquainted with their culture. They are more likely than Anglos to be stopped on the street and searched, offended in their dignity by rough questioning, and jailed for minor offenses or none at all.

So, instead of trying to be someone else, Chicanos are fostering pride in being what they are, even while they rub elbows with another culture. A Chicano told a visiting Mexican professor, "Within each of us a struggle goes on between Mexican and American ways, between corridos and rock 'n' roll, between tacos and hamburgers."

2
WHO AM I?

 CHAPTER 5

FIFTH GENERATION

JOE has a term paper to write—not a composition of two or three pages but something more ambitious, twenty pages perhaps. What matters most is not the length but the research. By research the teacher means digging out facts in the library or, even better, interviewing knowledgeable people and reporting what they say.

Joe, a Los Angeles High School senior, is at a loss. "Why don't you write about your family?" asks the teacher. "Find out where they are from and why they came to America."

An interesting idea. Joe has grown up with the idea that his family has always lived in Los Angeles or at least so long that he is as American as anyone. But lately things have happened to puzzle him. Only last summer he applied for a counselor's job at a children's camp, but when they saw that his last name was Gonzales, they said, "Sorry, but our counselors are all Americans. The parents would object to a counselor who wasn't white."

Now, actually, Joe is as light-complexioned as the man
who interviewed him, if that is what "white" means. He
passes unnoticed in the Anglo neighborhood where he lives,
and he's liked at school because he's a nice guy and adds
strength to the basketball team. Joe's father, though darker,
is on good terms with his neighbors. Not everyone in Los
Angeles is a bigot and, besides, Pepe Gonzales was a war
hero. In World War II.

Pepe is a nickname for José or Joseph, and Joe as the eldest
son bears his father's name. He has three older sisters. Two
are married to Anglos named Bellini and Litvak. Never mind
that these names don't sound very English. Anyone not Mexican American is Anglo. A Black, too, may be called an
Anglo, or at least a Black Anglo.

The third sister, Meche (short for Mercedes), is a *prietita,*
darker than the others. This didn't matter when she was
little, but in high school her girl friends began seeing less of
her and the Anglo boys didn't invite her to dances. She's now
married to Chente (Vicente) and lives in East Los Angeles.
Chente stands out even there for his coal-black beard. He was
with the Brown Berets in the 1968 and 1970 demon-
strations, shielding the smaller kids and absorbing the hard-
est blows when the cops got tough. He's taken the pledge:
"I wear the Brown Beret because it signifies my dignity and
pride in the color of my skin and race."

Joe had been too young for that hassle. He was ten during
the "blowouts," when Chicano high school students walked
out to protest that the curriculum failed to meet the needs of

the barrio. Besides, the schools involved were not where Joe lives but across town in the turbulent Eastside. Even more removed was the grape pickers' strike in the San Joaquin Valley, not to mention the confrontations in New Mexico over the Hispanos' claim to their ancestral sheep pastures, and the assembly of Chicano youths in Denver, when they took the name of Aztlán and proclaimed themselves "a bronze people with a bronze culture."

Back in those years, Joe was looking forward to junior high school. He was near the rung on the educational ladder where many Chicanos, perhaps half, drop out of school. They'd come into the first grade not knowing English. By the time they understood the teacher, they'd fallen behind in arithmetic and reading. And in high school the work would seem too hard for them ever to catch up. Joe's case was different. His parents spoke English, except to *abuelito,* his old grandfather. The neighborhood was English-speaking, too, and in due time Joe came to junior high school knowing so little Spanish that he took it as a foreign language—and, of all things, from an Anglo teacher!

By the time Joe reached the eleventh grade, Chente had married into the family. He was an impatient brother-in-law, always ready for an argument. "Don't be a *vendido,* a sellout," he'd insist in the heat of debate. "You're raza, man, be proud!"

Joe, a quiet type, would say, "Little by little the Chicanos are making it. Look at Julian Nava, a Ph.D. in history from Harvard and now on the Los Angeles Board of Education.

What he's done, others can do."

"Yes, let's take Nava," was Chente's rejoinder. "Do you know what they steered him into in high school? Courses in body and fender work! Man, did he have to fight the establishment to switch to the college entrance track! And Congressman Roybal, do you know about him? He had high grades in algebra, so his counselor advised him to try for something in electricity."

It's fine to be an electrical worker if that is what one chooses. But other choices should be open, too. A Chicano should have the same chance as anyone to attend college and qualify as a lawyer, a doctor, an engineer, or a professor. On this Joe and Chente are agreed. Where they differ is that Joe tends to see a career in terms of making good. That's due, Chente tells him, to having lived in the Anglo culture, with its emphasis on competition and personal success. Joe needs to work with MECHA and learn that for a Chicano a career is a way of helping his people.

MECHA stands for Movimiento Estudiantil Chicano de Aztlán. It's a federation of student groups that serve the barrios in various ways. One project encourages Chicano high school students to qualify for college entrance. Its activities include workshops and counseling sessions in the high schools, sometimes with special attention to girls, whose apprehensive parents may give their consent only if two sisters enroll together for mutual protection. Since promising students often lack fluency in English or are poorly prepared in note-taking, rapid reading, and study habits, they may need tutoring before and during college. Advanced students are recruited to supply this help in a spirit of *carnalismo,* or brotherhood.

Perhaps Joe, looking forward to State College, will be drawn into this movement. If he needs help less than some, he has more to give. Meanwhile, there's that term paper to write. Who were his people and why did they come to America? They must have come from Mexico, way back. But isn't Mexico part of America? Anyway, it will do no harm to explore his roots and it may help him to find out who he is.

 CHAPTER 6

FOURTH GENERATION

DAD, you know all about our family. When did we come to this country?"

Pepe Gonzales frowns. "We've been here a long time, son, longer than many of the Anglos. You were born in Los Angeles, as I was. Your grandfather missed being a native son only because his mother was temporarily across the border."

"And my mother's family?"

"They were in Texas when it was still part of Mexico. Ask her about them."

Joe's father doesn't classify himself as a Chicano or even a Mexican American. He says he's an American, nothing more and nothing less, as he's proved by fighting for his country in World War II.

"Before the war, though, weren't you raised in Mexico?" Joe was confused about this period. Pepe Gonzales explained that, yes, at the age of nine he'd been sent with his parents to Mexico. "Repatriation," they called it, though he and his

mother were United States citizens by birth and his father
had lived here most of his life. This happened during the
hungry depression year of 1933.

"The county figured the more people they shipped out, the
fewer mouths would be left to feed. *Cuando menos burros más
elotes.* Fewer burros, more ears of corn. As soon as I was eighteen, I returned with my birth certificate—just in time to
enlist after the attack on Pearl Harbor."

Pepe Gonzales has a Bronze Star and a Purple Heart but
doesn't talk about his own war record. He's immensely
proud, though, of the patriotism of "my fellow Americans of
Mexican descent," who volunteered out of all proportion to
their numbers. Heavily represented in combat divisions, they
were awarded seventeen Congressional Medals of Honor.

Joe gathers that World War II service did a lot for his father's generation. A third of a million Mexican Americans
saw a world outside the barrios and labor camps, many for
the first time. They mingled with Anglos in basic training,
faced common dangers in foreign lands, and grew in self-con-
fidence. After the war many went into the American G.I.
Forum or the Mexican American Political Association. Pepe
Gonzales, though not a joiner, did avail himself of the G.I.
Bill of Rights to get a home loan and to qualify as a dental
laboratory technician. This was a step up the ladder for the
Gonzales family, one that will make it possible for college-
bound Joe to climb another step.

But there's no honey without gall (*no hay miel sin hiel*). In
June, 1943, Joe's father was with the paratroopers in North

Africa, training for the invasion of Sicily, when news of the
zoot-suit riots in Los Angeles came as disheartening evidence
that prejudice was far from dead. The zoot-suiters, who
called themselves *pachucos,* were barrio teen-agers, cut off
from their Mexican roots and insecurely transplanted to
foreign soil. Inspired by the jitterbug craze in the East,
they'd adopted long-tailed dancing drapes of their own, tight
at the ankles, loose at the knees, wide at the shoulders, and
topped off with a ducktail haircut. They were an irritant to
the swarms of servicemen then in Los Angeles, waiting to be
shipped out and tense, bored, and battle-ready. Many had
never seen a Mexican American before. Surely, they thought,
anyone so costumed, and dark of face besides, must be un-
American! Minor encounters ensued and were not long in setting off a powder keg. Bands of men in uniform, on foot and
in commandeered taxicabs, roamed the barrios, looking for
zoot-suiters to beat up and disrobe. When none were to be
found, ordinary Mexicans served as victims, or Filipinos or
Blacks. The forays continued for several nights, giving the
country a bad name throughout Latin America and providing
grist for the enemy's propaganda mill.

Joe's Uncle Miguel was one of the victims. A brawny meat
cutter today, it's hard to see in him the frail thirteen-year-old
who was looking at a Gary Cooper movie thirty-odd years ago
when, suddenly, the house lights were switched on and the
sailors poured in, dragged him to the street, and stripped
him of his outlandish garb while photographers' bulbs
flashed. Miguelito was left bleeding from a broken nose. He

was picked up by a patrol car and booked on suspicion. That is the extent of his police record.

The following spring Joe's father was in Los Angeles on furlough. At a dance given by the Benito Juárez Society he met Teresita Mendoza's family. There being a war on, he was able to shorten the formalities and win Tere's hand before his leave was up. They were married upon his discharge. The Mendozas were from Crystal City, Texas, which they call Cristal, with the accent on the last syllable. They'd come to California to pick strawberries, then stayed to work at packing-shed and cannery jobs for which no Anglos could be found. Joe's Mama Tere remembers that it was much better than cutting Texas spinach on her knees for seventy-five cents a day—with all respect to Popeye, the statue, who stands there so vigorous on his Crystal City pedestal.

Then or later, lots of Joe's maternal kin left Texas for California. From them he is piecing out a picture of how things were during the war and afterward. As a wartime ally, Mexico supplied the United States with raw materials for industry and *braceros* to keep the trains running and the nation fed. Braceros were seasonal laborers recruited to relieve the labor shortage in the United States. During the war a quarter of a million Mexicans worked in a score of states. Despite poor food and irregular work, many returned each year to the same employer, glad to have a job at all.

After the war, the bracero program continued until 1964. More land was coming under irrigation, more hands were needed. If braceros were sometimes in short supply, wetbacks

were never lacking. When cotton was standing unpicked in
the late 1940s, wetbacks were hastily "dried out" and given
legal working papers. But when they became too numerous,
as in 1954, Operation Wetback was launched to speed the
unwelcome guests' departure. Braceros, then wetbacks, were
an inexhaustible source of cheap labor. They came to domi-
nate one crop after another: lettuce, tomatoes, melons, citrus
fruit—and lately the wetbacks have made inroads into the cu-
linary and clothing trades. They have become the Chicanos'
chief competition for low-paying jobs. Even so, Chicanos live
in dread of the periodic manhunts that turn the barrios up-
side down in the search for "illegals." Mistakes are made,
friends suffer, homes are destroyed as workers without documents are torn from their American-born families.

During World War II, Texas was a special case. Mexico
would not certify braceros for Texas, holding that their dignity as Mexicans suffered when they were refused service in
restaurants and barber shops and sometimes even denied the
use of public toilets. But many were hungry enough to swallow their pride and wade the Rio Grande. So numerous, in
fact, were the wetbacks in the border country, during and
after the war, that Tejanos began moving to Houston and
Dallas or, like the Mendozas, to California. Those who remained in South Texas came to regard it as a winter home.
Relinquishing the onions and spinach to the newcomers, they
spent much of the year with Colorado beets, Illinois aspara-
gus, Wisconsin cherries, and West Texas long-staple cotton.
Felix Longoria lies in Arlington National Cemetery. He died

in combat in the Philippines, but to the shame of many Americans, including Texans, he was refused burial in his home town of Three Rivers.

This Texas prejudice against his mother's people puzzles Joe. They assure him that things are better now. San Antonio has the welcome mat out for Mexican tourists, and they come all the way from Mexico City to shop at Joske's. The University of Texas has tailored a program to appeal to Chicanos at a new campus in San Antonio. Mama Tere wonders if she would recognize Cristal since La Raza began winning elections and improving its side of town. Even so, it's still an uphill fight. Though discrimination is not limited to Texas, it sometimes shows itself there with a virulence that suggests a fierce and ancient blood feud between peoples. Joe hopes to find out how it all started as he digs deeper for his own roots.

CHAPTER 7

THIRD GENERATION

Tere mendoza was a little girl during the Great Depression of the 1930s. What Mama Tere most remembers, she tells Joe, is San Antonio's Westside and her mother Rosario shelling pecans for four cents an hour to keep the children in school.

The Mendozas might better have stayed in the Winter Garden country clipping onions—except for the high school. Alonsito, their oldest boy, had finished the local "Mexican" school and had done so well that his parents tried to get him transferred to the "American" high school. But the idea of a Mexican in their high school was disturbing to the school board. As the chairman put it, "If we educate Mexicans away from their work, who will transplant the onions?" But since Alonsito's parents persisted, he finally told them, "If you must put your boy into high school, then go to San Antonio."

So Doña Rosario took her children and moved in with relatives in the city, while the senior Alonso went out seeking that almost unobtainable blessing called work. Rosario found that shelling pecans had its advantages. She could nibble on nutmeats and then say at mealtime that she wasn't hungry, for it was embarrassing to take much at the table while contributing little toward the household expenses.

"Your grandmother, may she rest in peace, was *sufrida* and *abnegada,*" Tere told Joe, meaning long-suffering and self-sacrificing, the qualities most admired in a mother. "She wanted her son to have a good education. And even me, her daughter. Not like at the Mexican school, where they taught geography without even a map."

The depression hit San Antonio exceptionally hard, there being no money for relief until federal funds were provided. The government also set up a labor board and told the pecan people they'd have to pay twenty-five cents an hour. This so horrified them that they put in shelling machines and let all the Texas Mexican women go. Tere remembers her mother saying there were ten thousand let out.

Tere's job-seeking father, meanwhile, was on the road, sustained by hope. But hope, during the depression, was like the laurels in a Mexican plaza—always green but never bearing fruit. Alonso went to the Colorado beet fields, only to find that footloose solos like himself were not in demand. The growers preferred contracting with a large family at so much an acre for all the handwork: blocking and thinning in the spring, then pulling and topping in the fall.

Many of the beet workers were from northern New Mexico. They called themselves Spanish Americans but they called Alonso a Mexican and were annoyed that Anglos couldn't tell them apart. Nevertheless, seeing Alonso destitute, they gave him food and shelter and addressed him as *paisano,* or countryman. The Spanish Americans were sheepmen by preference, but their herds had declined since the government began putting the ancestral grazing lands into national forests. To make out they had to work in the beet fields—and now the Okies were coming to compete with them!

The Okies were coming all right. They were farm folk from Oklahoma and adjacent states whose drought-stricken acres were being smothered in a bowl of dust. Alonso saw them heading west in the ancient *morelt\u00eds,* their Model T Fords, with top and running board piled high with cooking utensils, bedding, and unhappy hens. In the Arizona cotton fields, goaded by hunger, they worked in heat that, supposedly, no "white man" could take. They'd hire out at fifteen cents an hour, ten cents, anything at all, and there was nothing for Alonso. He followed the mirage on to California, and so did the Okies.

The thirties were a time of strife in the Golden State . . . small harvests and too many hands . . . hunger marches . . . short-lived labor unions with English and Spanish names . . . strikes that won small gains or were broken by mass arrests . . . blood on El Monte strawberries, Merced peaches, Salinas lettuce, Lodi grapes, Los Angeles celery.

Alonso, to his sorrow, was unable to send much money to

his family in San Antonio. After the pecans gave out, the Mendoza family went back to South Texas for better or worse. Alonso was hardly aware that he had changed, but the Anglos knew. They had a saying, "Beware of a Mexican who has been to Los Angeles." And though Alonso politely removed his hat when talking to them in the field, they sensed that he did not do it as quickly as before. So they were just as happy when, during the war, he went with his family to California to stay.

Don José, Joe's other grandfather, experienced only the opening phase of the depression in the United States, for afterwards he was in Mexico where hard times were normal. He never got over the indignity of being sent out of the country on a special train, for which the county paid at $14.70 a head, as if people were cattle. That is how Don José and his American-born family were "repatriated" to a country none of them knew. He himself had been born on the Mexican side of the Rio Grande by the mere happenstance that his old-fashioned mother preferred being attended by a Ciudad Juárez midwife rather than by an El Paso doctor. No one in those days cared about comings and goings at the border. Yet a generation later, they became important enough to uproot a family.

Never, after his return to Los Angeles years later, did Don José trust anyone connected with the government, not even the public health nurse who came to see about the grandchildren's shots. "No spik inglés," he'd say, despite being bilingual since his childhood on El Paso's South Side. When

Pepe came home with a Bronze Star, Don José admired his son's courage but was unimpressed by the decoration. "So what?" he asked. "Can you eat it?"

Mama Tere reserved a place in her heart for her crusty father-in-law. "He's a devil," she'd say, *"pero es más diablo por viejo que por diablo,* he's more of a devil for being old than for being a devil." Pepe agreed. He remembered his own eight-year exile in Mexico as a boyhood adventure. But to his father it was a wound that never healed.

The old man thought of himself as a pioneer who'd given his youth and health to California's Imperial Valley and helped transform it from a desert into the nation's largest food basket. At eighteen he'd left El Paso and the black cop-per smelter where his father sweated and had put down roots in an outdoor inferno where summer temperatures rise to 117 degrees in the shade—"only there's no shade." There, in the new and booming Imperial Valley, he built himself a brush shelter on the banks of an irrigation ditch and swung into a yearly round of picking cotton, harvesting lettuce, planting cotton, cutting alfalfa, picking cantaloupes, cleaning ditches, and back to picking cotton. July was cotton-chopping time. The men, under a gang driver, chopped out the superfluous plants, each on his row, not walking but trotting. Anyone falling behind was very visible. At the end of the row each man belly-flopped and drank a gallon of irrigation water from the ditch. Never mind the mud. It was drink or die.

July, 1930, found José a family man in his thirties, still chopping cotton. It was a young man's work, his wife tried to convince him, but he replied, *"Soy muy aguantador,* I have great endurance"—and kept on till he suffered sunstroke.

That was when the family moved to Los Angeles. Don José found work as a gardener and was able to set a slower pace and be more in the shade. He made a down payment on a duplex, thinking it would provide some rental income, but the depression worsened and he was unable to keep up the payments. And then came the blow from which he never recovered: deportation to Mexico.

Don José, reminiscing for his grandson's term paper, is very old now. He recites his disappointments freely, but only in Spanish, and is irritated when Joe does not immediately understand. "Why do you function only in English? You say it is the language of the country? Our people have no country. Look at me. The best of my life and strength I leave in this country. And what do you see before you now? A broken old man. Perhaps some day we shall have a country. Perhaps it is the destiny of your generation to give us one. But first you must know who we are. Learn our beautiful language, *mi nieto,* my grandson, learn it well, never forget it, and use it proudly!"

CHAPTER 8

SECOND GENERATION

Iɴ her time, Don José's mother Concepción (Joe's great-grandmother) knew the virtues of many herbs, besides potent prayers for curing *susto,* or fright, and other illnesses. "Once," Don José recalls, "a visiting neighbor woman took me in her arms and said what a good-looking little fellow I was. In doing so, she unintentionally put the evil eye on me. At least that is what my mamá thought, so she took an egg and rubbed me all over with it, real hard. Then she broke the egg into a saucer and put it under my cot, letting the evil pass into the yolk."

Doña Concepción had a neighbor who complained of *duendes,* elf-like creatures seldom seen but fond of nighttime pranks like pulling off the bedclothes. The way to make them leave was to burn palm leaves that had been blessed on the Sunday before Easter. However, Doña Concepción could not be bothered. There were no duendes in *her* house. What would induce them to come from her native village in Guanajuato all the way to El Paso? But her neighbor replied that duendes become very attached to a household and are hard to shake off. She herself, when she came to the United States, was already on the second-class coach with all her bundles and cooking pots when she remembered she'd forgotten the broom. "Don't worry," piped up an unseen duende. "We're bringing it."

One might laugh off duendes but not *ánimas*. These latter were souls in pain, fated to wander between this world and the next, looking for someone to make good a vow they'd failed to keep—like offering a one-peso candle to the saint of their devotion for a favor received. They drew attention by their ghostly wailing, and a passerby who did them the requested charity might be directed to a hidden bag of coins as a reward. It was dangerous, though, to spend the treasure except on the poor. Otherwise the finder might sicken and waste away.

The most fearful apparition, most people agreed, was the Devil, whether in the form of a black dog or a horseman in a silver-buttoned riding habit. However, Don José's father— they called him Don Chepe—remained unimpressed. After working around reverberatory furnaces at the smelter, no threat of the Devil could frighten him, he said. His concern was the Mexican Revolution.

Joe is curious to know more about his great-grandfather Chepe, and Don José searches his childhood memories. Don Chepe, being a railroad man's son, was in touch with the train crews that laid over in Ciudad Juárez and gave them bundles of the underground paper *Regeneración* to be smuggled into Mexico. Sometimes little José himself would go with a basket of *pan dulce* to sell to the passengers—and under the sweet rolls were the papers he was waiting to slip to a trustworthy switchman. In Mexico the copies were passed from hand to hand until they were in tatters. Those who couldn't read listened to those who could. Nearly every future leader of the Mexican Revolution knew *Regeneración,* and one of them was to say, "It lit a flame that will never be extinguished."

The paper was edited, now in St. Louis, now in Los Angeles, by Ricardo Flores Magón and his circle of refugees from the tyranny of Porfirio Díaz. The Díaz dictatorship dated from 1876, "the year my father was born," says Don José. Since then, Don Porfirio had dispossessed a million families of their little farms and village lands and reduced them to debt slavery. Those who ran away were pursued by the rural police and returned to peonage or "shot while trying to escape." The more educated people, the ones in high collars and bowler hats, were favored with small government jobs, because, said the dictator, "A dog with a bone neither bites nor barks."

Flores Magón, too, had a saying, "Nothing is sadder than the sight of a contented slave." He visited El Paso in 1906 on a revolutionary mission, coming from St. Louis, where he had presided over an organizing session of the Mexican Liberal Party. Its program called for labor and land reforms like those now embodied in the Mexican Constitution. But a long struggle lay ahead, and Flores Magón was too often in prison to lead it to victory.

Four years later, a refugee junta in San Antonio proclaimed Francisco Madero as Mexico's president. And soon Madero—with Pancho Villa in the forefront of the fighting—took Ciudad Juárez and put Díaz on the run. Don José, then thirteen, watched the battle from El Paso and heard how the kindhearted Madero had led the captured enemy commander over the bridge to safety on the American side. Madero's chivalrous conduct was not repaid in kind two years later when the counterrevolutionists struck back and brutally assassinated him. Before 1913 was over, though, Villa rode into Ciudad Juárez at midnight in a captured train and raided the gambling houses for gold coins with which to buy American arms. Now that the Revolution had a port of entry opposite El Paso, it entered a new and fiercer stage. It went on till 1920 and beyond, while Carranza, Villa, Obregón, and Zapata made common cause or had their fallings out. Each of them met his tragic end while the Mexico of today was being born in pain.

Mexican immigration to the United States was at flood tide during the Revolution, World War I, and the booming 1920s. These people became the root stock of much, though not all, of today's Mexican American population. Young José, before going to California, saw the first wave rolling over the bridge into El Paso, jammed into the little streetcar, coming on foot, lugging suitcases, carrying babies in black shawls, guiding burros laden with roped bundles and caged birds. A few rode in *Fotingos* (Fords) or bigger cars recalling better days.

Not all the newcomers were of as humble origin as they looked, for the revolutionary convulsion uprooted people of all political factions and every station in life. Some were remnants of broken armies, including farm laborers who had shaken off their ancestral debts and had no place to go back to. Some were shopkeepers whose towns had become battlefields or lay in the path of pillaging armies. Those who had become embroiled in political intrigues, particularly on the losing side, found it wise to flee their neighbors' wrath. A few had owned country estates that now were blackened ruins, but unless they had ready cash they would soon be picking cotton. Those with a profession or a trade were no better off. Unable to work at their highest skills, they had no choice but to sign with a labor contractor to work in *el fil* (the fields) or *el traque* (the railroad tracks). And the contractor, a man who knew his way around in two languages, collected their wages for them, making generous deductions for his trouble.

Into the great labor market of El Paso poured an unending stream of the displaced from battle-ravaged Chihuahua and Zacatecas and the highlands of Guanajuato, Jalisco, and Michoacán. "Stoop labor," it was called, bending to strip from snowy bolls the cotton lint so much in demand for automobile tires and wartime uniforms. Cotton was spreading over the Texas cattle country and the Southwestern deserts, wherever water could be brought to the land. When cotton prices collapsed after World War I, fruit and vegetables took up the slack. People turned to salads, greens, and a more varied diet. Canneries multiplied, and yards for drying prunes and raisins, while lettuce now sped to market in iced cars. Agriculture began changing into what is now called "agribusiness."

During the war, or soon after, Joe's maternal great-grand-father on the Lower Rio Grande gave up the lariat for the grubbing hoe in order to chop brush. He rubbed shoulders with refugees from the Mexican countryside north of Monterrey and Saltillo and together they rid the thorny land of mesquite and prickly pear and created the Texas Winter Garden.

In World War I, Mexican Americans, and Mexicans too, served in the armed forces as volunteers and conscripts. One man, perhaps typical of others, was puzzled to understand why "I was refused service at a hamburger stand but drafted into the United States Army."

The war having shut off European immigration, Mexicans were recruited in San Antonio and El Paso, and even in Mexico, to work in the North and East. They lived in boxcars, worked on the tracks, or went on to the Michigan beet fields, the Chicago stockyards, and the steel mills of South Chicago and Bethlehem.

Don Chepe, for his part, yearned for breathing space, now that El Paso was a vast labor market and his children were growing up and leaving home. Stories of a copper boom and high wages drew him to the Arizona mining camps. But what he found there aroused the old revolutionist in him. His people were largely restricted to unskilled labor, and the few who did advance were paid less than Anglo miners for the same work. To speak up in protest in these company-owned towns, as he did, was branded as unpatriotic and ample cause for being roughed up or run out of town. *"Fuí por lana y me trasquilaron,* I came for wool [money] and they sheared me," he is said to have remarked shortly before he died in a mine accident.

CHAPTER 9

FIRST
GENERATION

J OE'S grandfather remembers *his* grandfather as Pa Grande. This was another way of saying *abuelito* in the ancestral village in Guanajuato from which the family came. Don José's personal recollections, however, reach back only to his childhood in El Paso, where his grandfather would stop over while waiting to ship out on a job.

Pa Grande was a railroad man. Not an engineer or a conductor—such jobs were closed to Mexicans even on the American-run lines of their own country—but a tracklayer, a section hand, sometimes a cattle loader. Pa Grande accepted his destiny cheerfully. "I take what they give me," he'd say. "If they are pears, I eat them; if they are stones, I pile them up." (*Yo como me las dan las tomo. Si son peras, me las como; si son piedras, las amontono.*)

"Nowadays we'd call him a Tío Taco, an Uncle Tom," observes Don José. "Still, in 1884, he must have felt pretty good to earn seventy-five cents a day after a long stint of forced labor in Mexico."

Early in 1884, in Zacatecas, Pa Grande had helped drop
the final rail in place on the Mexican Central right-of-way,
thereby linking Mexico City with El Paso. An earlier Mexican president had opposed the project with the warning,
"Let there be a desert between the strong and the weak."
Porfirio Díaz, however, allied himself with the strong and
gave the railroad builders subsidies and unlimited forced
labor at twenty-five centavos a day.

Pa Grande was one of innumerable villagers who toiled
with pick and crowbar in Mexico, then crossed over at
Nogales or Laredo, or more often at El Paso, to continue the
work they'd come to know. Many signed with the Santa Fe
Railroad, the Southern Pacific's rival for the California traffic.
Formerly the Chinese and the Irish had been the railroad
builders; now it was the Mexicans.

Pa Grande was with the crews that carried the Santa Fe
line over the Mojave Desert and through Cajon Pass into Los
Angeles. They advanced, army-like, with mobile huts and
tents, clearing yucca and chaparral, grading, filling, bridg-
ing, dropping ballast, laying ties, unloading rails, gauging,
spiking, bolting. Once the trains rolled into Los Angeles, a
rate war with the Southern Pacific was on. Tourists came
west by tens of thousands, many remained, and the City of
the Angels was never the same again.

Pa Grande worked there as a car cleaner in 1887, the year
of the Great Boom, when real estate prices skyrocketed and
orchards as far south as Fifth Street were cleared for building

lots. But he felt more at home in Sonoratown, near the Plaza, where the whitewashed adobes, pack-burro trains, and flocks of sheep reminded him of Mexico. Sonoratown was then changing into Chinatown, and his people were spreading into new barrios. As yet not many were from his part of Mexico. Rather they were children of Sonora miners or grandchildren of Californio cattlemen who had been lords of the range when the first Yankee trappers entered California like wetbacks. Now the ancestral Mexican ranches were passing into new hands as a result of drought, title disputes, and lack of ready cash for paying unaccustomed land taxes. Pa Grande bought his tamales from a ruined Californio who had lost 3,000 acres by foreclosure.

No one remembers all the places where Pa Grande worked after 1887 and on through the 1890s. But the labor market was in El Paso and from there he shipped out on six-month contracts, often to New Mexico, to judge from his stories. When possible, Ma Grande went with him to prepare his tortillas, and they and the children lived in boxcars, traveling with the job, or in section-houses that would fix the location of future barrios.

New Mexico was largely Spanish-speaking, but its Spanish had the antique flavor of another age, like the tales told there of grateful animals, cruel stepmothers, and headless horsemen. Every gentleman knew how to compose a pretty couplet when requesting a dance, and he could accompany himself on the guitar while singing a ballad beside a campfire. People were fond of riddles, for example: "Up in the Sangre de Cristo mountains, a shepherd saw what God cannot see. What was it?" Answer: "The shepherd saw another shepherd, but God did not see another God."

They were shepherds, especially in the Upriver country, and they ran their flocks on the customary pastures of their ancestors. But now Texas cattlemen, enclosing land for ranches, were stringing barbed wire in the path of the flocks. The aroused sheepmen complained, *"Con el alambre vino el hambre"* (With the wire came hunger). Now and then, when matters came to a boiling point, the Gorras Blancas (White Caps) would assemble secretly and ride through the night, cutting wire and slaughtering the hated longhorns.

The sheepmen also turned their wrath against the railroads for bringing in these Anglo intruders with the promise to ship their cattle and produce to market. Everywhere the railroads were changing old ways for better or worse . . . opening forests to lumbering, stocking ranges, carrying freight, writing finis to the wild freedom of the Apaches, opening the Spanish Southwest to an Anglo tidal wave. The Butterfield stage that had crossed the plains in twenty-four days now belonged to the past. There was machinery in New Mexican silver and copper mines that had been shipped around the Horn to the Gulf of California and freighted overland by mule teams. Now it came in on flatcars. Already California oranges were being shipped to New York. The Golden West could feed the nation, given water for irrigation and plenty of Mexicans to climb, stoop, squat, and do the drudgery.

Joe is mulling over this background. He has followed the thread of his family into the past as far as he can—back four generations in his father's line—and he suspects it was earlier still when his mother's family came into Texas with their cattle. The Chicano people were pioneers of the Southwest, blazing trails, founding pueblos, opening mines, creating farm and pastoral wealth, laying rails and highways, building cities and airports, and putting their hands to every task. They have made great contributions to the nation and now ask the right to make the even greater ones of which they are capable.

Joe knows that though he has the makings of a term paper, it is not yet the whole story. Chicano roots go deeper still. They draw sustenance from ranchos and missions, Hispanic cowboy ways, ancient pastoral villages, incredibly bold explorers, Old World antecedents, and—who knows?—from ancient Mexico before the Spaniards came. It remains to uncover these chapters and draw proper conclusions. This is a task for college and another reason for attending.

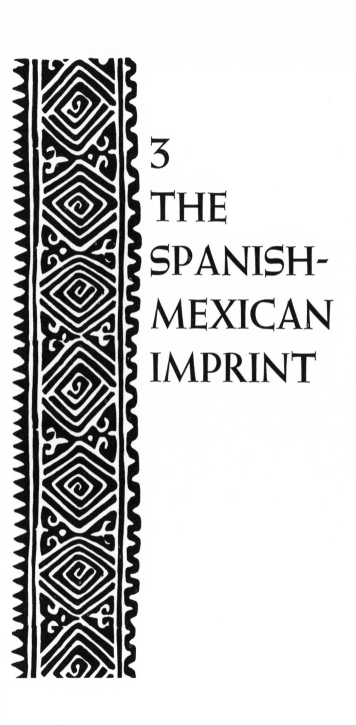

3
THE
SPANISH-
MEXICAN
IMPRINT

CHAPTER 10

BEFORE THE
FORTY-NINERS

ORO," murmured an Indian laborer, using the Spanish word for gold. He'd worked in Mexican mines elsewhere in California and recognized the *chispas,* the gleaming flakes, that his foreman James Marshall was cradling in the crown of his hat. Marshall had just fished them from the tailrace of a sawmill he was building on the South Fork of the American River. News of the find, spreading by pack train and sailing vessel, was to draw a hundred thousand forty-niners to the Sierra streams.

Before the forty-niners came the forty-eighters, mostly Spanish-speaking. The discovery took place on January 24, 1848, nine days before California passed from Mexico to the United States under the Guadalupe Hidalgo peace treaty. Gold mining had been going on along the California coast since 1842, when a Mexican herdsman made a strike near Los Angeles. But the rich inland deposits along the mountain streams were then unknown except to Indians who placed

59

little value on yellow pebbles. However, the native California Mexicans did prize them and were close by when the rush began. Nor were Mexicans from Sonora far behind. They came humbly attired in sandals and white cotton but wise in mining lore. They used the *batea,* a flat-bottomed wooden bowl, washing the pay dirt in it, then separating the lighter sand from the particles of gold. If water was lacking, as often it was in the dry diggings below Sacramento, they tossed the mixture into the air and relied on the wind, or their own lungs, to blow the sand away.

Upstream from the placer mines, where the gold was loose, were ridges where it came encased in quartz and could be freed only by milling. Under their broad-brimmed sombreros the Sonorans carried the know-how for making a simple mill called an *arrastre.* It consisted of a paved enclosure with an upright post to which a beam was attached. A mule, hitched to the beam, dragged a block of granite round and round over the quartz until it was pulverized. After that, the gold was extracted by amalgamating it with quicksilver, which came from the great New Almaden mine near San Jose.

Though more Spanish-speaking gold-seekers arrived from Chile and Peru in 1849, they were greatly outnumbered by Anglo-Americans who crossed the plains or came by sea. Friction developed, as will be told, and "foreigners," including native Californians, were forcibly expelled from many of the bonanzas, or rich strikes, they had taught others to exploit.

The gold rush drew Americans of every sort—rich man, poor man, beggarman, thief—into back country sparsely peopled except by Indians. Yet the newly established camps were soon operating under miners' codes regulating the size of claims and the conditions under which they could be worked and retained. California historians, like my scholarly cousin Owen C. Coy, may he rest in peace, used to attribute this happy state of affairs to "the extraordinary capacity of the Anglo-American for self-government." But it is now well established, by Carey McWilliams among others, that the forty-niners, having little mining background of their own, turned to laws and customs that had been tested by centuries of experience in Mexico and Spain. From California they were to carry throughout the West the Hispanic principle that property in mines depends on discovery and development. Mining law in the United States rose on these foundations.

Mexican labor was in heavy demand as mining became big business. Ore-carriers with hide sacks climbed from pits with 200-pound loads suspended by straps from their foreheads. Mexican smelter men were rated tops around the copper mines which, later on, were to supply an essential metal for electrification. Their skill went back to the Spanish-discovered Santa Rita mine in western New Mexico, where basic copper mining techniques were evolved. It was a Mexican who first recognized that Nevada's Comstock Lode was fabulously rich in silver. He could have been from Sonora, where his countrymen had been mining silver since 1763.

Silver had been drawing men north for three centuries, and

the Sonorans' ancestors no doubt had mined it in Sinaloa and Guanajuato. Earlier, the conqueror Cortés told the Indians, "We Spaniards suffer from a disease of the heart for which gold is the only cure." But Mexico's silver far exceeded her gold and was in fact so abundant that for two centuries the Spanish dollar, or more correctly the Mexican peso, was a preferred currency in the Far East, the Caribbean, Africa, and much of Europe. It was legal tender in the early United States. When Paul Revere needed silver in his shop, he melted pesos.

In sixteenth-century Mexico, a forty-niner would have been one of the fortune-seekers who in 1549 were rushing to Zacatecas, the site of a recent silver strike. Zacatecas became a roaring silver camp and the point of departure for points farther north. Within twenty years, the mining frontier moved into Durango, Coahuila, and Chihuahua. The recovery of silver was stepped up tremendously after a Pachuca miner had the inspired idea of treating the crushed ore with quicksilver. *Arrieros,* or mule drivers, moved freight over long stretches of lonely, arid country by pack train, an art that remained of utmost importance in Mexico and the Southwest until the railroad age. Stock ranches supplied the mines with work animals, food, and hides for cables and sacking. Lucky prospectors became *ricos mineros,* mining magnates, and *señores de ganados,* cattle lords. A few rose to be governors of provinces, and nearly all assumed the military title of *capitán.* In far-north Chihuahua and Sonora, however, pretensions of wealth and power were less in evidence. Rich and poor needed one another for protection from Indians whose nomadic life style was threatened by colonization. Here on the mining frontier, a mixed-blood Mestizo (usually more Indian than Spanish) was *todo un hombre* if he was a good man.

By the end of the eighteenth century Mexico had three thousand silver mines, besides scientific institutions, including a School of Mines which Baron Humboldt, the scientist who visited Mexico in 1803, considered without equal on the new continent, not excluding the United States. All this was in the line of a Spanish mining tradition, unbroken since ancient times when seagoing vessels carried Spanish tin to the Bronze Age civilizations of the Middle East. Mexico's miners and metallurgists carried this tradition into the Southwest, contributing their skills and the sweat of their backs to the growth of the United States.

 CHAPTER 11

THE FIRST COWBOYS

THOUGH a century has passed, the movie cowboy on his sure-footed mustang, a lariat at his saddle, still drives his yearlings over the long trail to the railhead at Abilene, Kansas, where Wild Bill Hickok represents what there is of law and order. After returning to his outfit, he rounds up calves for the branding pen or tames broncos, digging his knees into the wild critters' flanks while waving his ten-gallon hat to prove he's "a buckaroo who don't pull leather."

In the world's eyes, nothing is so American as the cowboy. His image was formed between 1867 and 1885, when millions of Texas longhorns served to supply Eastern markets and to stock new ranges all the way north to the Dakotas and Montana. Then came hard times. Drought and blizzards took toll of the stock. Barbed wire barriers put an end to the long drives. A new era of windmills and fenced enclosures began. But a brave age lives on in the Westerns of story and screen. It is an American epic with a Spanish accent. The cowboy is

64

heir to the *vaquero,* a word which came through to him as buckaroo. His lariat was *la reata.* His chaps, affording protection from the chaparral, were *chaparreras* or *chaparejos.* His ten-gallon hat, seemingly named for its size, was inspired by the Mexican cattleman's *sombrero galoneado,* which was galooned with adornments like gold lace. His half-wild mustang was a *mesteño.* Light-bodied and fleet, his mount justified the Mexican saying, "Praise the big ones but put your saddle on the little ones." The mustang was in large part a Spanish horse, whose remoter ancestors included Barbs from the North African deserts. Fatter cattle have replaced the longhorns, but Spanish strains still run strong in Western horses.

The Spanish-Mexican influence has persisted, too, in items of horse gear, including the saddle with a high horn around which the cowboy dollies or dolly welters the rope after lassoing an animal. Dolly welter is from *dale vuelta* (give it a twist); lasso from *lazo,* a slip knot. A rodeo is an exhibition of animal-handling skills, but in the days of the open range it was a roundup, where cattle were separated according to their outfits and calves were branded with the *fierros* their mothers bore. Disputes were settled by cattle judges, or *jueces del campo,* representing the cattlemen's associations, which came down from the powerful *mesta,* representing the livestock interests of early Mexico and Spain. As for the elements of the brand markings—bars, circles, crosses—who knows their age? Some, with their sunbursts and crescent moons, could be as old as Moorish Spain.

Cattle raising, as best known in the United States, began in a strip of lower Texas between the Nueces and the Rio Grande. It was thorn brush and prairie grass country in the nineteenth century, and the inhabitants lived under five flags, those of Spain, Mexico, the Texas Republic, the United States, the Confederacy, and again the United States. It was at times a Comanche hunting ground and often a no-man's land where smugglers, bandits, and cattle rustlers plied their trades. After 1836, Texas "volunteers" periodically invaded it to make up for losses suffered in their independence fight. Later on, Mexican *tuvos* rode in "to take back grandfather's cattle." Since *tuvo* means "had," a tuvo was one who had had property and been deprived of it.

Raids led to reprisals, with the Comanches helping one side or the other for their own good reasons. In the face of growing disorder, the Mexican rancheros pulled back to the Rio Grande towns and the stock ran wild.

This was the disputed country in which war between Mexico and the United States broke out in 1846. After the war, Americans with capital to invest came and organized great ranches, stocking them with the wild cattle and hiring skilled and seasoned vaqueros. Incoming Anglo hands adopted the practices of the country and the language of their craft in translation or in mangled Spanish. They became cowboys like the vaqueros. The great herds multiplied during the Civil War when access to the Mississippi Valley was shut off. Afterwards they were a seemingly inexhaustible source of the nervous, leggy animals that were driven over the long trails to new markets and unstocked Western ranges.

This narrow pocket between two rivers that inspired our cowboy culture first became range country in the mid-eighteenth century, when José de Escandón, last and most peaceful of the conquistadors, founded the Spanish province that was to be the Mexican state of Tamaulipas. Rather than establish a garrison, he settled the land with soldier-colonists. Also he brought in families of Tlaxcalan Indians, traditional allies of the Spaniards, to teach the local Indians how to use seeds, tools, and domestic animals. The Rio Grande became the chief thoroughfare of this colony, and soon it was shipping cattle to New Orleans and the Caribbean. The first towns were on the southern bank, but Laredo was founded on the north side before the American Revolution. In 1776, if not before, Blas María Falcón started a ranch at the mouth of the Nueces. He was the great-great-grandfather of Cheno Cortina, who, as we shall see, became a Chicano folk hero.

These frontier ranchers, unlike the cattle lords in deeper Mexico, worked beside their cowhands, to whom they were often related. Their sons and grandsons frequently continued to hold the ancestral land in common. Gradually the Indian vaqueros and sheepherders were absorbed into the blood and culture of the Spanish settlers, as the Texas folklorist Américo Paredes has pointed out. The Rio Grande people lived a simple, rather idyllic life, or so it must have seemed to anyone looking back from the troubled years between 1810 and the late 1870s.

California, like Texas, reckoned cattle in the millions,

especially in the southern "cow counties," of which Los Angeles was queen. But the industry was brought to the brink of ruin after 1862 by droughts and land title disputes. Moreover, California was so remote from markets that, until the gold rush, beef was practically a giveaway. A beef animal was valued for its tallow and hide. Tallow was used for soap and candles, while hides were in demand by the Yankees who made shoes in Massachusetts. In *Two Years Before the Mast,* Richard Henry Dana, Jr., describes a voyage around Cape Horn to pick up "California banknotes," as hides were called. The skipper paid for them by selling notions from Boston, including crockery, tinware, tall combs, silks, calicoes, and four-dollar shoes often made from the buyers' own leather. Dana brought his prejudices with him and deplored the bare arms of California women and the frequent holy days when no work was done. "There's no danger of Catholicism's spreading in New England," he wrote. "Yankees can't afford the time to be Catholics."

The two years referred to in Dana's title were 1834 to 1836, when the California mission lands, with their herds and flocks, buildings and workshops, and docile Indians were passing from the custody of the Franciscan fathers to a few score wealthy rancheros. Their golden age lasted until the gold rush in northern California and a little longer in the cow counties. They maintained great households of relatives, hangers-on, and Indian servants, counted their cattle in six figures, and thought nothing of spending three thousand pesos for a hand-tooled saddle with silver mountings. Travelers enjoyed their princely hospitality and were given horses and servants for the next leg of their journey.

If the rancheros were more lordly than their Texas counterparts, the vaqueros were more lowly. Indian, at least on their mother's side, they were swift riders, deft in slaughtering cattle on the run with a well-placed knife blow on the neck. Others followed, stripping off the hides and cutting up the meat for salting. They cured the hides in brine, stretched, scraped, and dried them, folded them hair side in, and delivered them in wooden-wheeled carts to be put aboard ships at Santa Barbara or San Pedro, or perhaps at San Diego, where the first cattle were brought ashore when the city was founded in 1769.

Familiar to cowboys everywhere were the roundups or rodeos. Mexican colonial records of the sixteenth century describe vaqueros with their iron-tipped prods bringing in the animals for sorting and branding. Only seventeen years after the Conquest, in 1538, the herds were multiplying prodigiously on the virgin range. Beef was cheaper than bread, but cattle were a menace to the Indians' unfenced cornfields. Before mid-century, outfits of 150,000 animals were common. The thundering herd was moving north in the wake of the mining frontier. Already it was on its way to Texas and to immortality in Hollywood.

CHAPTER 12

NEW MEXICO, FIRST HOMELAND

WILL ROGERS, cowboy humorist of an earlier generation, once said that the New Mexicans could have sent a committee to welcome John Smith to Jamestown. Indeed they could, and with nine years to spare, for it was in 1598 that the first Spanish colony was planted in the Upper Rio Grande Valley. Santa Fe was founded in 1610 and is still capital of New Mexico. Spanish surnames in that region go back fifteen generations and more. When the United States took over the sparsely settled Southwest, four-fifths of the Spanish-speaking population lived in New Mexico. They numbered some 60,000, compared with 7,500 in California, 5,000 in Texas, and 1,000 in Arizona. The mark they have left is lasting and deep.

For many lifetimes New Mexico seemed to be at the end of the world, separated from the heart of Mexico and even from its Texas and Arizona neighbors by mountains, deserts, and hostile Indians. Every two or three years a caravan reached

Santa Fe, escorted by soldiers, after six months en route from Mexico City by way of the mines. It was easier for New Mexicans to trade with Chihuahua, though that city lay six hundred miles down the river and over the Jornada del Muerto, the waterless Dead Man's March, then past the site of El Paso, and across still more deserts. Pack trains and carts left in the fall with buffalo hides, beaver pelts, woolen blankets, salt, turquoise, and flocks of sheep. After five months they returned with chocolate, silver-studded horse trappings, satin waistcoats from Spain by way of Veracruz, and silks from China via Acapulco. These luxuries were for the *ricos,* the rich folk, not for people who spun their own wool, milled wheat and corn for their tortillas, and lanced buffalo on the plains.

Money was scarce. A bereaved family might offer a bull calf for a funeral mass. A horse was priced in terms of buffalo robes. A yearly fair was carried on by barter at Taos in the Rio Arriba or Upriver country. To it came Hispano settlers, Chihuahua merchants, and Indians from the pueblos and plains. Comanche warriors offered hides for hatchets and traded captive children from enemy tribes for handloomed cloth. The purchased children worked in Hispano households and they, or their children, came to consider themselves Spanish. After Mexico became independent, Yankee mountain men appeared in Taos, offering furs for gold dust and entertainment. By this time the Santa Fe Trail was open, and Missouri merchants were freighting piece goods, oil lamps, and tableware to the New Mexican capital. They returned

with furs and buffalo robes. Alongside the freight wagons
walked strings of New Mexican mules, such as are still
famous as Missouri mules. Before long, the more ambitious
merchants were trading to Chihuahua and beyond and marrying into influential Santa Fe families.

Influence was frequently a measure of the number of sheep
a family possessed. Though the first Spanish settlers had
brought sheep into New Mexico, it was not until late colonial times that ranches numbering their flocks in hundreds of
thousands began spreading over the Rio Abajo or Downriver
country below Santa Fe to set the pattern of Western sheep
raising. Under the *patrón,* or owner, were the *mayordomo,* who
managed the ranch, and the *caporales,* who rode between the
camps, keeping them supplied. Lowliest and loneliest were
the *pastores* or herdsmen, who moved with the seasons between the winter range and the high meadows. They led
their flocks to shelter in time of storm and kept fires burning
when it turned cold during the lambing season. The shearing
was done by specialists who rode from ranch to ranch, bringing with them a taste for music and ballads that enlivened
the summer nights. The fleece, combed, carded, tied, and
loomed, gave employment, among others, to Navajo women,
whose descendants were to make the blankets that are now
collectors' items.

The sheep were *churros,* lean, scrubby animals from Mexican range land too poor for cattle. The name is not compli-
mentary. *Churros y charros,* for example, are Class B Mexican
Westerns that ring in everything from these ugly sheep to

handsomely costumed charro riders. But the churros could endure heat and cold, and a ewe of the breed would defend her lamb from a coyote. They were originally from Spain, like the woolly Merinos with which later they were crossed. Sheep raising continued to prosper under American rule and spread onto the Western plains. There Hispano sheepmen met cattlemen from Texas, and a not always peaceful contest for the range ensued.

Though a score of *rico* families were lords of their sheep and sheepmen and a power in the land, they were not all of New Mexico. Others had more modest holdings, while in the Upriver valleys were villagers who made out with a plot of corn, beans, squash, and red chiles, and a few head of stock. Spain, and later Mexico, had made land grants, large and small, to draw settlers to a remote frontier and reward soldiers for duty in hostile Indian country. Often a grant was made not to an individual but to a colony or a village. Each family then received a home site and a farm plot, while the pastures, woods, and waters were reserved for common use. Even private holdings were apt to change into communal villages from the need for mutual protection. Incoming farmers and artisans might be allowed to buy into the land and run sheep on the commons. After a generation or so, their descendants would be intermarrying with the founder's grandchildren and combining their flocks.

The Hispano custom of holding certain lands in common stemmed from Spain and Mexican Indian practices, but was to cause deep misunderstanding when the Anglos came with more rigid ideas of land ownership. But another old Spanish custom lives on in the community property laws of several Western states, by which a wife shares equally with her husband in property acquired after their marriage.

Laws concerning water rights also show the Spanish touch. English tradition holds that every property owner has a right to the undiminished flow of any stream crossing his land. But in the arid Southwest, irrigation would be impossible without fairly apportioning what little water there is. Hispano farmers, from the beginning, organized water users' associations after the customs of Mexico and Spain. They made their rules and elected a *mayordomo* or ditch boss to enforce them and to settle disputes. They took turns keeping the *acequia madre* or mother ditch in repair, and every man knew when he could take water from it and how much.

The Southwest has changed since those times, but water is still scarce. When the public authorities allocate it for irrigation, electrical power, or a city's water supply, they ask, "What is the most beneficial use?" This guideline on dry-country water rights stems from the experience of Mexico and Spain.

So precious was water that the line of settlement in New Mexico followed the Rio Grande and its tributaries. In the low-roofed adobe villages, on the dusty plains, or in the high valleys under the shadow of pine woods and snow-covered mountains, lifeways changed slowly. The villagers, all cousins or compadres, greeted one another with a *buenos días les dé Dios* (may God grant you a good day). At bedtime children kissed their parents' hands and received a blessing.

A fiesta was an occasion for dancing, storytelling, and light-hearted songs about a land of plenty where tortillas grew on trees and anyone who worked got a whipping. In everyday life New Mexicans were sober folk, admired for their weaving and for silver candlesticks and plate.

Santeros carved *santos,* or figures of the saints, from cottonwood root and colored them for the churches. People were on familiar terms with their saints and knew their quirks. If a mule strayed, San Cayetano would find it if one first laid a small bet that he would be unable to do so.

There were times, however, when religion put on a grimmer face, especially among the Penitentes, lay brothers who aided the destitute, comforted the dying, and gave themselves over to rigorous penances in their windowless *morada,* or chapel. On Good Friday eve, they went in procession up a hill, wearing black hoods, dragging chains, and lashing their backs with yucca whips until the blood flowed. Amid chanting and the wail of flutes, some brothers pulled a death cart in which sat Doña Sebastiana, a dressed female skeleton with bow and arrow poised to shoot. One chosen brother dragged a heavy cross to the hilltop. There he was tied to it with horsehair rope. Then the cross was raised, and he remained on it as long as he could bear. Such forms of devotion were brought from sixteenth-century Spain and have persisted in traditional New Mexico villages where old ways seem better than new.

The Hispanos have always had Pueblo Indians as neigh-

bors. The two cultures have interacted for nearly four centuries. Many Pueblo villages have been absorbed or abandoned, but those remaining cling to their life styles in
speech, art, music, kinship terms, and religious ceremonies.
The first Spaniards found the Pueblos living in many-tiered
apartment buildings and keeping turkeys, not for Christmas
feasts but to have feathers for dance costumes. The Pueblos
were hard to change. Even after accepting baptism, they continued offering prayer sticks in their underground kivas and
teaching their young men the masked kachina dances. To
discourage these practices, Spanish officials burned the masks
and whipped the medicine men. For the Pueblos, already
paying tribute in goods and labor and normally the least
warlike of Indians, this was the last straw. In 1680, under
the medicine man Popé, they staged a bloody uprising and
sent the survivors fleeing to Paso del Norte. A dozen years
passed before the Spanish conqueror Diego de Vargas began
recovering the lost territory.

Over the generations, despite strained relations, there was
a mingling of customs and blood. Some natives went to live
with the Hopis and Navajos or died of smallpox. The settlers
who replaced them included Mestizos from Mexico and Plains
Indians who had been freed from Apache captivity. Where
old ways fell into disuse, villages became Spanish in culture,
or rather made out with a combination of native farming,
Mexican stock raising, and Spanish tools. They built stone
and adobe houses with projecting roof beams in the Pueblo
style, but added doors, windows, and fireplaces. And they

dined, Spanish style, on tamales, pinto beans, green chiles, and wheat tortillas in the northern style, though only the wheat was originally Spanish.

Many of the soldier-colonists who came to New Mexico in 1598 with the Zacatecas silver magnate Juan de Oñate were *españoles mexicanos,* or Mexican Spaniards. Spanish in culture and mixed in blood, they had an affinity for the northern frontier, where courage counted for more than a family tree.

New Mexico had received its name in the hope that it would be another Mexico, rich in treasure like the conquered Aztec capital. A more pressing reason for pushing so far north in 1598 was Francis Drake. Some years before, the English privateer (a pirate in Spanish eyes) had rounded Cape Horn and plundered the Pacific coast. The Spaniards, surprised to see him there, imagined he must have sailed from ocean to ocean by some secret passage north of New Mexico. After the defeat of the Spanish Armada, it was feared that the English might come that way and try to seize the Mexican mines. So the Oñate expedition marched north from Chihuahua: officers in coats of mail, soldiers in buckskin, Franciscan missionaries in robes and sandals, carts laden with flour, horseshoe nails, and other staples, and several thousand head of stock. Upon reaching the Rio Grande, Oñate flung stones in the four directions and claimed New Mexico for Philip II.

Oñate's father and father-in-law were founders of Zacatecas and immensely rich. His wife, Isabel de Tolosa Cortés Moctezuma, was a granddaughter of Cortés and a great-granddaughter of Moctezuma. She was not less Spanish for an Indian ancestor, especially one so distinguished. She was Spanish because she lived in the style of a great Spanish family. No doubt some of Oñate's armored knights, and later settlers as well, were wholly Spanish by ancestry. Did their descendants remain so down the generations? The belief that they did runs strong among some prominent families, especially since New Mexico became one of the United States with their emphasis on the importance of being European. But generally speaking, Latins are less inclined than Anglos to pigeonhole people by race or ancestry. A Mexican definition of an Indian is "one who lives like an Indian." A similar logic shows up in the modern Southwest, for example, when it makes Anglos of men named Bellini and Litvak. Realizing these facts, some New Mexican students with Spanish surnames now speak of their Indo-Hispano culture. To go on calling themselves Hispanos or Spanish Americans, they feel, is to deny part of a proud heritage. And if the term Indo-Hispano sounds too fancy for everyday use, why not, they ask, just say Chicano?

 CHAPTER 13

EXPLORERS AND PATHFINDERS

A FEW weeks after the Boston Tea Party, Capt. Juan Bautista de Anza, who knew nothing of the event, blazed the first overland trail to California. From Tubac, south of Tucson, he led a military party over the uncharted desert to Mission San Gabriel. Then he returned and conducted 240 colonists, half of them children and several born on the way, over the new route and up the coast, where he founded San Francisco in the memorable year of 1776.

Spanish settlement in Upper California went back only to 1769, when a party coming by sea joined another from Lower California and established Mission San Diego. Twenty more missions were to rise farther up the coast to San Francisco and beyond. Today, with their bell towers, red tile roofs, and cloistered walks restored, they are enduring symbols of Spanish and Mission California. Gone, though, are the great flocks and herds and the Indian converts, learning the tasks of weaving room, wine press, and blacksmith shop, and the an-

swers to the catechism, all at the proper hours as regulated by
bells. Hardly a remnant of the Mission Indians remains, but
the fruits the friars introduced—peaches, apricots, plums,
cherries, grapes, olives, figs, apples, pears, lemons, and
oranges, besides walnuts and almonds—are California's pride.
Some were a thousand years on the way from Persia and
Egypt to North Africa and from there to Spain, Mexico, and
California.

Fray Junípero Serra lives on too, in memory, as California's
patron saint. Zealous founder of the early missions, he expected much of the Indians and more of himself. On his mission rounds he limped from an infected scorpion bite which,
he said, *"no es cosa de cuidado"* (is nothing to worry about).
The missions, along with military posts like those at Mon-
terey and Santa Barbara, made California Spanish at a time
when the Russians were moving down from Alaska.

Mission San Gabriel was the place where overland travelers
came out on the fruitful coast. Forty-four Sonora and Sinaloa
colonists gathered there in 1781 to establish a pueblo nearby,
which they named for Our Lady, the Queen of the Angels.
People called it Los Angeles. Everybody rested at San Gabriel
after the desert crossing. Jedediah Smith's band of Yankee
trappers stayed there in 1826, prophetic of things to come.
But the rancheros from Mexico were the immediate challenge
to the old ways. As their herds multiplied, they looked with
envy on the spacious mission lands, so well supplied with Indian labor. The Indians were supposed to have a share of the
land as they became self-reliant Christians. But after two

generations they were too weakened by disease and schooled in obedience to hold their own in the political strife that brought the mission era to an end. Most of the land passed into private hands after 1834. The Indians became ranch hands and servants or took refuge in the sierra, where the gold rush completed their ruin.

California was known before it was explored—and named before it was known. The coast was familiar to mariners returning from Manila to Acapulco and had been explored by Sebastián Vizcaíno in 1602 and Juan Rodríguez Cabrillo in 1542. Even then California was a magic word on Spanish lips, for a romance of chivalry, a best seller of 1510, named it as an island near the terrestrial paradise, abounding in gold and precious stones and ruled by women warriors called Amazons. The conquistadors considered California well worth discovering. The Indians they questioned said the Amazons sounded like the brave women who had died in childbirth and become, according to their old beliefs, an honor guard to the setting sun. So Spaniards, Cortés among them, looked in the West and found a peninsula which they named California and believed to be an island.

California, then and long after, meant chiefly Lower California. Father Eusebio Francisco Kino, a Jesuit missionary, was there in 1685. Having a scientific bent, he noticed some blue seashells on the coast. Later he was assigned to the Pima country along the present Arizona-Sonora border. One of his fifty or so journeys of exploration took him in 1699 to the meeting place of the Gila and Colorado rivers. There he was given some blue shells like those he had seen on the Pacific coast. Since they had come here by land in the course of trade, California could not be an island. Father Kino is best remembered in Arizona for the San Xavier del Bac Mission near Tucson but he founded many others, besides planting orchards, stocking ranches, and teaching arts as varied as mule raising and the violin.

In the normal course of events, prospectors and ranchers followed the missionaries. An Indian riding a horse was, in Spanish eyes, like Eve eating the forbidden apple. After the 1680 Pueblo revolt, however, many Spanish horses fell into Indian hands and spread to the plains, where they proved a fantastic boon to the buffalo hunt. The good tidings reached the Comanches in Wyoming around 1700, and they came into Texas for horses, pressing on the Apaches, who found new hunting grounds in the western border-lands. By the 1760s the Apaches had become a scourge to everyone who posed a threat to their way of life. They would raid stock ranches and destroy mines and settlements, then scatter into the hills. For more than a century they were a barrier to travel between Santa Fe and the settlements in California and Texas.

Texas, a year's pack-train journey from the Mexican capital, was valued as a bastion for the defense of the silver mines, which Spain was ever fearful of losing. As the French came down the Mississippi and began exploring the Gulf Coast at the end of the seventeenth century, the Spanish countered with missions and military posts in eastern Texas. Few of these were permanent except San Antonio, established as a stopover point in 1718. When Spain resumed control of the Louisiana country by treaty in 1762, Texas appeared quite safe. But the English were traditional enemies and so, during the American Revolution, Spain came in on the colonists' side. Bernardo de Gálvez, for whom Galveston is named, wrested Natchez, Baton Rouge, Mobile, and Pensacola from the English, thereby making it easier for the fledgling United States to keep the Illinois country that George Rogers Clark had taken.

Spanish surnames are woven into the warp and woof of American history. When Pocahontas was married to John Rolfe at Jamestown, Diego de Molina was present, though not by choice. He was a Spanish grandee, taken prisoner while spying out what the English were up to so close to Florida. It was then a century since Juan Ponce de León had come to Florida, looking for treasure and the fountain of youth but fated to die from the wound inflicted by an Indian arrow. Others coming to Florida were to fare no better. Lucas Vásquez de Ayllón went on to South Carolina and died of fever. Pánfilo de Narváez perished in a Gulf storm. Hernando de Soto, setting out from Florida, discovered the Mississippi River and the country beyond before dying from the hardships of his long journey. The first to establish a permanent settlement in Florida was Pedro Menéndez de Avilés. In 1565 he founded St. Augustine, which alone among United States cities is older than Santa Fe.

Seventy years before Santa Fe was founded, Francisco

Vázquez de Coronado, not yet thirty, led an expedition from
the west coast of Mexico to New Mexico and the Seven Cities
of Cíbola, where the doors, it was said, were studded with
turquoise and there were whole streets of silversmiths. They
did not live up to their billing and were in fact unpretentious
Zuñi pueblos. Neither were the Rio Grande pueblos a new
and richer Mexico. The explorers' excessive demands for treasure led to an Indian uprising, and Coronado burned many
prisoners at the stake. The survivors were only too happy to
see him off over the plains to Quivira, whose king was said to
nap under a spreading tree to the tinkling of golden bells. In
Texas and Oklahoma the party saw herds of buffalo, which
they called "hump-backed cows covered with frizzled hair."
Not until reaching the thatched huts of the Wichitas in central Kansas in 1542 did Coronado turn back, his last illusions
gone. Before him was the thankless task of explaining his
costly failure to the viceroy. It was small consolation that he
had explored so much of the United States and that one of his
parties had discovered the Grand Canyon, whose pinnacles
were "higher than the tower of the Cathedral of Seville."

What had first kindled interest in the Southwest was an
eight-year-long journey on foot across the continent by four
castaways dressed in animal skins. Members of the ill-fated
Narváez expedition to Florida, Alvar Núñez Cabeza de Vaca,
two other Spaniards, and a Black Moor named Estebanico
were all who survived out of four hundred. Shipwrecked on
the Texas coast in 1528, they reached Sinaloa in 1536. They
kept alive by living with Indians and like Indians. In one
place, they might be cared for tenderly; in another, held in

servitude to dig roots. Cabeza de Vaca mastered several languages and engaged in trade between coastal and inland
bands. He and his companions were all but forced into the
role of medicine men ("physicians without diplomas," in
Vaca's words). Besides blowing and sucking in the Indian
manner, they made the sign of the cross and said an Our Father in Latin. Estebanico, with his gourd rattle and expres-
sive black face, was particularly impressive. The travelers
gained such a reputation for curing that multitudes accom-
panied them between the campsites and villages. From the
Texas coast their route lay up the Rio Grande, with wide de-
tours to one side and the other through country unknown to
Europeans. They were told of buffalo in the North, where
turquoise was to be had for parrot feathers, but chose to leave
the river at El Paso and seek the western ocean. Beyond
mountainous Chihuahua they came into Sonora and passed on
to the Sinaloa River, where they met their own countrymen
after eight years.

Vaca's joy at reaching this frontier was short-lived, for the
Spaniards were slave-hunters, laying waste the country and
taking captives to work in the mines. The horror he felt
showed how much he now identified with the people who
had seen him through his hungry wanderings. Most painful
of all, as he later wrote the king, was to recognize in the
slave-catchers the Spanish *caballero* he himself had been eight
years before. Is it too much to say that Cabeza de Vaca, early
wanderer in Aztlán, and Spanish yet also Indian, was a pioneer Chicano?

CHAPTER 14

FROM SPAIN
WITH HONOR

INTO the Southwest from Mexico came mustangs, long-horns, muskets, wheat bread, guitars, the written alphabet, and much more, not forgetting old-time Spanish ideals of honor, dignity, and fortitude. If these ideals are universal, their expression depends on the time and place. During the Moorish wars, El Cid rode into battle with his beard tied up, for to have it pulled would have been an unbearable affront to a warrior's honor. Don Juan Tenorio, who figures as a great lover on the Spanish stage, learned this the hard way. After betraying a grandee's daughter and then killing him in a duel, he desecrated a mortuary statue of his victim by pulling at the sculptured beard. Don Juan realized he had gone too far only when he felt the stony grasp of the statue's hand, pulling him down, down, into hell.

Cervantes tells of seagoing gentlemen who fell captive to Barbary pirates rather than stain their honor by putting a hand to the galley oars. For the same reason, Cortés had trouble manning the brigantines he used to attack the lake-girded Aztec capital. But however highborn his men might say they were, he made them go and row.

Concepts of personal honor and dignity, nourished in the long struggle of Christians and Moslems for mastery of Spain, reached a fierce intensity during the sixteenth and seventeenth centuries, the very time when Spanish colonists were coming to Mexico. Many of their children and grandchildren were to go on north and populate the borderlands.

In these crucial centuries, Spanish soldiers occupied a New World empire, and Spanish sailors circumnavigated the globe. It was the Golden Age of Spanish literature, marked by *Don Quijote* and a brilliant theater. Spain itself was a stage where men of spirit and passion—warriors, saints, kings, zealots—played their heroic and tragic roles.

"Let us build a church such that future centuries will believe we were mad," they'd said in Seville while planning a cathedral to replace the old mosque. Religious fervor was subsequently to run even higher than that. Two sons and a daughter of sixteenth-century Spain became famous saints. Iñigo López de Loyola, while recovering from battle wounds, searched his soul, mortified his body, and became founder of the militant Jesuits. San Juan de la Cruz (John of the Cross) was a mystic and poet. A nun once asked him if his words came to him from God. The saint replied that sometimes they did and sometimes he had to look for them himself. He collaborated with Santa Teresa de Jesús in reforming the Carmelite order. They wore sandals or went barefooted, believing that the soul finds union with God only through suffering and penance. Santa Teresa had three warts on her plain face but was able to stir others to the depths. She would interrupt her prayers and cross half of Spain in rain and snow, by mule or cart, to open a new convent. A certain innkeeper, knowing her reputation for austerity, expressed surprise at seeing her eat two partridges with relish. She told him, "Penances are penances, and partridges are partridges."

The penances that saints imposed on themselves were notable for their rigor. Even ordinary people were urged to subjugate the flesh to the spirit. They joined religious brotherhoods, observed fasts, practiced self-mortification, and prepared themselves for a good death. Today religious devotion takes other forms. New Mexico's Penitentes are now apart from the mainstream, yet who, better than they, have faithfully preserved traditions inherited from sixteenth-century Spain?

That century, at its most fanatical, spoke with the voice of Philip II. He was an unsmiling king, who made his court dress in black and, in his last years, ruled his empire from a monk's cell. Spain's well-being, he believed, demanded religious unity. In his youth he took Mary Tudor, England's Catholic queen, for his bride. She was short-sighted and sickly and had a mannish voice, but the fleet that carried Philip to his wedding was bright with banners and painted sails. A union of the two crowns, he hoped, would halt the spread of heresy. Grimly he told his suite, "I am not going to a festival but to a crusade."

But no heir came of the marriage and, when Mary died, Philip entered upon a long struggle with Elizabeth I. He enforced religious unity at home with the Inquisition's help and refused to spare his own father's godson, telling him, "If my son were as evil as you, I would myself carry the wood to burn him with."

These were not tolerant times. Miguel Servetus, the Spanish doctor who discovered the circulation of the blood between the heart and the lungs, missed the Inquisition by leaving Spain. But his Unitarian principles were equally abhorrent to Protestants, and he was burned in Geneva by John Calvin's authority.

Those most gravely suspect in Spain were the New Christians, that is, Jews and their children who had accepted conversion or had it thrust upon them. They were very numerous. Some sought a new life by going to Mexico and on to the borderlands, and their blood flows in Chicano veins. But most stayed in Spain, and it is surprising how many scholars and churchmen were New Christians. Even Teresa the saint had a Jewish grandfather. Fray Luis de León, Bible scholar and Salamanca professor, was of similar background. This did not help him when he translated Solomon's *Song of Songs* into Spanish verse. For the song treats of love, and the Inquisition feared it would be understood in a worldly rather than in a spiritual sense. The learned friar spent five years in prison before he cleared himself and returned to his lecture hall. "Well, gentlemen," he began, playing it cool, "as we were saying yesterday . . ."

Spaniards of humble state expressed their dignity in say-
ings like *Mientras en mi casa me estoy, rey me soy* (Within my
own house I am king). There were even high churchmen who
challenged unlimited royal power. Bartolomé de las Casas
defended the Indians and opposed wars of conquest, while
Francisco de Vitoria, one of the founders of international law,
held it to be a subject's duty to refuse to take part in a war he
considers unjust.

Honor remained the supreme Spanish value but ceased
being the exclusive possession of the highborn. A commoner
could gain honor by his deeds, declared the Mexican-born
playwright Juan Ruiz de Alarcón. Spain's greatest dramatist,
Lope de Vega, in *Fuente Ovejuna,* praised the honor and dignity of a peasant village that rose against a villainous military
commander.

This has been a glimpse of the Spain that sent many of her
sons and not a few of her daughters to the New World. They
came especially from sheep and cattle country where the hills,
they say, are so bare that a bird can hardly find a place to
light. In similar surroundings in Mexico some rose to be
cattle lords and proudly asserted, *"El rey está lejos; aquí mando
yo"* (The king is far away; here I give the orders). Even the
propertyless had strong notions of honor, dignity, and fortitude. These qualities have made Elfego Baca a Chicano hero.

Elfego Baca, peace officer and mayor of Socorro, New Mexico, around the turn of the present century, is best remembered as the curly-haired youth of nineteen who stood off
eighty Texans in a gun battle in 1884. He was in the

Spanish-speaking settlement of Frisco, making campaign speeches, when a drunken cowhand came riding down the street, shooting at passersby in a spirit of fun. This was not an unusual occurrence. The man belonged to an outfit that was a law unto themselves and thought Sundays and holidays were meant for celebrating in saloons and frightening "Meskins." Elfego warned his Hispano friends that matters would only get worse unless someone imposed order. As no one seemed to want to, young Baca appointed himself a deputy sheriff, arrested the trigger-happy Texan, and prepared to take him to the jail at Socorro.

A Texan arrested by a man named Baca! A call went out for reinforcements to punish such presumption and free the prisoner. But Elfego told himself, *"No te rajes"* (Don't get cold feet), and when the smoke cleared, thirty-three hours later, four Texans were dead. Most of the time Baca was under siege in a *jacal,* a mud-and-pole shanty. A mob numbering eighty poured four thousand shots into the flimsy structure. They turned the door into a sieve and almost collapsed the building with a dynamite charge. Baca was not touched. He owed his charmed life to three things. He placed his Stetson hat on a holy image of Santa Ana (St. Anne) to draw the fire away from himself. He was protected by the floor's being below street level. And anyone who approached came in line of his unerring aim.

After two days and a night, a real deputy arrived, a truce was arranged, and Baca came out with a six-shooter in each hand, just in case. He was twice tried for murder and twice acquitted and he earned his people the grudging respect of the Texans. In middle life, when Elfego Baca was a prominent attorney, he always kept his gun within reach and, though portly, could whirl like a flash, if need be, to face an enemy. In a gun fight, he said, if one is to be buried and one to be tried, it is better to be the one who is tried. He died in bed at eighty.

4
ANCIENT
INDIAN
LAND

 CHAPTER 15

TWO-WAY ROAD

IF Joe Gonzales studies Mexican and Southwestern archaeology at State University, he'll find he's more than a fifth-generation American. For thousands of years his New World ancestors moved freely about the Southwest and Mexico "like Peter in his house" (*como Pedro en su casa*), as the saying goes.

During the original peopling of the Americas the traffic flow was mainly from north to south. Hunters were passing from Asia to North America over a now submerged land bridge before the Ice Age ended. They spread over Canada and the United States and some of them pushed on to Mexico and beyond. Campsites more than twenty thousand years old have been reported in Mexico. Ten thousand years ago, men armed with stone-pointed spears were hunting mammoths in the Valley of Mexico.

A hundred languages were spoken in Mexico when the Spaniards came. The most widespread of these belonged to the Uto-Aztecan family. One was Náhuatl, the Aztec tongue. Others of this family were spoken to the north along both sides of the Western Sierra Madre and on into the Southwest and the Great Basin of the United States. All may stem, according to linguists, from a common speech in use some five thousand years ago along the present Arizona-Sonora border or no farther away than New Mexico or southern California. From this linguistic Aztlán, migrant bands presumably carried their language to new hunting grounds or imposed it on people with whom they mixed. Over centuries and millennia the mother tongue split into dialects and separate but still related languages.

These were lean years, for after the Ice Age came heat and drought. The mammoth vanished, as did the big-horned bison and the American horse and camel. Hunters still dreamed of white-tailed deer but settled for jackrabbits. Everyday dry-country fare included roots and pods, cactus fibers that wore the teeth away, and, above all, the seeds of wild plants.

Fortunately, seeds carried an unexpected bonus. In the Tamaulipas highlands, pumpkin, bottle gourd, and chile pepper seeds were being intentionally planted as early as 7000 or 6000 B.C. A little later, and four hundred miles south near the Puebla-Oaxaca border, squash and avocados came under cultivation. Here, or in some similar place, a wild grass was domesticated about 5000 B.C. It put forth a tiny ear bearing only a few kernels but was the ancestor of Indian corn. Not much to look at and not yet an important food source, it nevertheless was to make civilization possible in the New World, as wheat and barley would do in the Old.

A dry mountain valley in south central Mexico is a surprising birthplace for such an important crop. Here, though, seed-gatherers could become seed-planters with only a pointed stick to break the ground. The rain—what little there was—came in the growing season. The food quest didn't take the band so far afield that a conscientious woman couldn't keep an eye on her kitchen garden. For food raising originally was women's work and no doubt an invention of women. A midget ear of corn must have been a good conversation piece. We can imagine women giving seed samples to their sisters in other bands. This could have been one of the ways by which the cultivated grain spread slowly to Bat Cave in New Mexico, a few miles from where young Elfego Baca was to have his gun battle five thousand years later.

Thus, after an age-long, north-to-south movement of hunter-gatherers, a feedback started. Mexican influences began infiltrating the North. It was not so much a migration as a spread of ideas, hastened later on by traders and merchants and perhaps by priests and war captains.

A thousand years before Christ, red kidney beans reached New Mexico, little known at first but rich in proteins for a population becoming too large to depend on game. The pace of development quickened about 500 B.C. when a more productive variety of corn arrived after a long passage from Mexico. The new corn grew tall and sent forth larger ears as a result of patient seed selection in its homeland and crossings with other varieties and related wild grasses. It was the staff of life in central and southern Mexico, where people had long since settled in villages to raise corn and show respect for the mysterious powers that sent the rain and made the earth fertile.

This new lifeway spread, slowly at first, in New Mexico and Arizona. Two or three centuries before Christ, villages appeared: huddles of roofed pit houses and, later, huts of pole, mud, and thatch. The villagers learned to make clay jars and bowls, as well as female figurines that were perhaps a form of magical crop insurance through woman power.

Pottery styles from diggings afford hints of the routes by which Mexican influences reached the Southwest. The most important ran along the base of the Western Sierra Madre's inland slopes. Less arid than the deserts to the east, it passed beyond a cultural frontier in Zacatecas and Durango into Chihuahua and the Southwest. By A.D. 500, strong impulses were coming over this pathway from Mexico, not in an unbroken flow, but relayed from point to point. They are revealed in the styling of ear adornments, for example, or by the pyrites mosaics that served as mirrors. Cultivators who tapped the Gila River for irrigation gradually lengthened the canals until they were miles long and brought water not only to the cornfields but to the cotton that was loomed into cloth. So impressive are the remains of this ancient system that modern Phoenix is named for the mythological bird that rose from its ashes to a new life.

In the centuries preceding A.D. 1100 or 1200, Mexican culture rolled into the Southwest in successive waves, represented by ballcourts with markers and rubber balls, temple mounds and forecourts, carved stone tablets, shell trumpets, and religious art depicting the earth mother, sun and star symbols, double-headed serpents, eagles, jaguars, and coyotes, and the four cardinal directions with their respective colors and gods. Another route was open now, from Nayarit and Sinaloa up the west coast. Over it, among other things, came little copper bells for dancers to tie to their wrists and ankles.

Other regions also felt the Mexican touch. Shortly before the Christian era, corn was spreading eastward. Mexican-type temple mounds were rising in the valleys of the Mississippi and its tributaries a thousand years later. Mexico, showing the way to civilization, was for a long time the mother country of much of the United States.

The people who came upon the secrets of agriculture and farmed Mexico's best land were, however, a favored few. They drew upon themselves the envy of desert wanderers and marginal farmers whose scraggly cornstalks withered in the frequent droughts. Coming from farther north in Mexico, these hungry folk, known as Chichimecs, broke into the charmed circle in the twelfth and thirteenth centuries and made themselves rulers. They learned the arts of civilization but only after central Mexico had passed through a century or two of confusion.

The Southwest was also troubled, not by Chichimecs but by hunters from the north, the ancestors of the Apaches and Navajos. To make matters worse there was a severe drought from 1276 to 1300, as shown by the narrow rings of tree growth for those years. Many pueblos in northern New Mexico and Colorado, remembered for their great cliff dwellings, were abandoned. Communications between Mexico and the Southwest were cut at various points by these calamities but not entirely halted. Figures resembling the plumed serpent and the Mexican rain god appear in Pueblo art and may be akin to the masked kachina dancers that were to distress the Spanish missionaries of a later century.

The Spanish occupation of northern Mexico, including the Southwest, was in a sense a resumption of the old surge northward from central Mexico. Among the soldiers and colonists who followed their Spanish captains were many Indians, including Tlaxcalans, Tarascans, and some of the conquered Aztecs. Others were Mestizos, whom Andrés Molina Enríquez later described as a strong and hardy blend of all the Indians, modified by the Spaniards—and seasoned, he might have added, with the part-Indian descendants of African and even Asian bondsmen. Náhuatl, the Aztec language long used in trade, was carried beyond its old frontiers into new areas of the North.

Only the rain god no longer went with the warriors, having been given up for St. John the Baptist and other Christian saints and Virgins. The greatest saint of all, as time went on, was Our Lady of Guadalupe—La Morenita with her dark face—who had appeared to the humble Juan Diego, promising in his Aztec tongue to help the Indian people in their sorrows and calamities.

The spread of Indo-Hispanic blood and culture into the Southwest was slowed, as we know, by an Apache barrier.

Then, during Mexico's internal convulsions following independence, the Anglos came into Texas and soon after won
all the Southwest. But despite the new management, Mexicans kept coming, to build railroads, mine copper, and pick
fruit and, in latter days, to press garments and assemble elec-
tronic components. It is an odyssey, thousands of years long,
of a people who never left home.

 CHAPTER 16

MESOAMERICAN MOTHERLAND

WE are Indian, blood and soul; the language and civilization are Spanish," wrote José Vasconcelos, an early twentieth-century Mexican philosopher. Perhaps the civilization, too, is more Indian than he realized. The British archaeologist Glyn Daniel counts the Valley of Mexico one of seven regions where the world's first civilizations appeared. And from ancient Mexico comes much that is typically Mexican—and hence also Chicano.

Cradled in a volcanic niche high in the mountains, the Aztec capital of Tenochtitlan had been spreading over land and water for two centuries when the Cortés party came to see, conquer, destroy, and rebuild it as Mexico City. The Valley of Mexico was an "eagle's nest" to the wandering Aztec founders. For their home they chose an island in one of its shallow lakes. The site was accessible by canoes and later by causeways equipped with drawbridges. As the city grew, temple pyramids rose over a gleaming white skyline of houses and palaces. On the fringes were verdant "floating gardens," built of matted water plants and rich lake mud and anchored by slender willows. The waterways threading the island were lined with houses, as were the causeways and the mainland shore.

To the Spaniards the city seemed to rise from the water as in a romance of chivalry. Some of them had been soldiers in Rome and Constantinople, but the parks and aqueducts, the canoes coming and going, the monuments, and the thronged marketplaces left them amazed. So did Moctezuma's palace with its marble halls and great plazas. Unknown in Europe was anything like the botanical gardens, with their flowering trees and medicinal plants, and the zoos with specimens of all animals, birds, and reptiles known in the land. Just one day's ration for the birds of prey was five hundred turkeys.

The conquistadors were surprised to find the streets cleaner than those of Europe. A thousand men stayed busy sweeping and cleaning them; not a straw of litter was to be seen. People had a curious and surely dangerous custom of bathing often. Moctezuma, in fact, took two baths a day! Every barrio had its school for boys and girls, while in the temple center a college-like Calmécac trained priests and high officials. Painted books like folding screens contained the pictures, numbers, calendar signs, and glyphs that opened the store of recorded knowledge. The glyphs called to mind objects, ideas, or syllable sounds and held the promise of a complete system of writing, something the Mayas, farther south, had already achieved.

The Spaniards found Aztec rule established from coast to coast and from the northern deserts to the green tropics. They called this vast territory an empire, though it stemmed from a confederation of three Valley cities, which then expanded through treaties, royal marriages, and conquest. The Aztecs have received little enough credit for their achievements but are remembered and much blamed for cutting out the hearts of war prisoners on the sacrificial stone. This emphasis on what was considered an honorable death overlooks how war prisoners were treated elsewhere. In medieval Europe those too poor to pay ransom were lamed, blinded, or slain. Cortés, reporting from Mexico to the king, mentions human sacrifice only in passing and then as hearsay. But his companion in arms, Bernal Díaz, writing in old age, recalls altars in every village reeking with blood. The story had grown with the years and the need to excuse the cruelties of the Conquest. Human sacrifice is found in the background of many other nations, including pre-Roman Britain and Spain. Yet a Los Angeles County law enforcement official, as recently as 1942, warned his men to take no chances with Mexicans, whose desire "to kill or at least to let blood," he asserted, "has come down through the ages," transmitted apparently from Aztecs to Chicanos!

The cruel-Aztec image fades when one considers their delight in flowers and jades, their gracious manners, and their tender feelings toward children as recorded by missionaries and native historians. A mother calls her daughter "my dove, my little one." To her father she is "my blood, my color, my image." Sorrowfully they confide to her, their precious turquoise, that she has come to a world of pain and fatigue, where she will bend over the metate and toil at the loom and the spindle. Her mother counsels her to shun gaudy clothing and painted lips and not to raise her voice or stare at strangers. If one day someone speaks for her, she will do well to take and hold on to him, even if he is a poor soldier or a ruined noble.

"My eagle, my ocelot, my son," says the father, "be not vain or proud." He calls the boy a precious feather, born of a noble family, but reminds him that one does not live by nobility alone. He should plant an orchard, sow the field, learn feather working, and perhaps some day he may be designated for a public office.

For teaching good manners there was a list of don'ts. Don't repeat gossip. Don't step in front of others. While visiting relatives, see what needs doing and don't look on while they work. Don't show disappointment over a small gift. While eating, don't squirm and wiggle. Don't eat with all your fingers; only three fingers—and use the right hand.

Tenochtitlan had grown into a prosperous city in the highlands under the volcanoes by practicing the sterner virtues. Fearful of the younger generation's growing soft, parents compared life to a narrow path over a mountain peak with an abyss yawning on either side for the unwary. Yet life was not all weeping, not while there was laughter, sleep, sustenance, strength, work, and the search for a mate. That is what parents told their children.

In the evening, boys and girls decked themselves with flowers and danced in the House of Song to the drum, flute, and rattle. Dancing blended with poetry and song. It was theater, too, as when youths costumed as birds and butterflies climbed trees to sip nectar from the blossoms and dodge pellets from the hunters' blowguns. Poetry was called Flower and Song and, as Miguel León-Portilla explains, it included art and the symbols through which man speaks perhaps the only truth there is on earth.

The vigorous young Aztec civilization was cut off in the bud, less than a century after Tenochtitlan was set up as an independent city-state. Carrying memories of a homeland they called Aztlán, the Aztecs had fought their way to the top, earning renown as warriors. They nourished their tribal god Huitzilopochtli, who symbolized the sun, with blood from their ear lobes and later from the hearts of their prisoners. He rewarded them with the spoils of war: gold and chocolate, shimmering quetzal feathers, costly red capes, and breech clouts with embroidered ends. Homage was paid to many gods, including Coatlicue, the mother of them all. She is the earth who gives life and takes it away, and her figure in stone, with its skirt of writhing serpents, is a masterpiece of sculpture.

The maturing Aztec civilization of later days had room for doves as well as hawks. Poets turned from gods who live on blood to a Giver of Life who creates himself (or herself, being also female) and who is everywhere but cannot be seen or touched.

Of this monotheistic belief was Nezahualcóyotl (Hungry Coyote), king of Texcoco, Tenochtitlan's ally, and a notable law-giver, poet, philosopher, and engineer. He was in the sixth generation of descent from a Chichimec chieftain who invaded the Valley dressed in animal skins. Those of his line who came after learned to sleep in houses, cook their meat, plant corn, eat tamales, wear cotton, enjoy music, and sponsor the arts. Nezahualcóyotl's culminating genius was a demonstration of Mesoamerica's power to civilize.

Mesoamerica is an archaeologists' name for a large area in central and southern Mexico and part of Central America whose people took up a settled life and came to share calendar systems, painted books and hieroglyphic writing, ballcourts, markets using chocolate beans for money, and religious ideas like associating the plumed serpent Quetzalcóatl with the rain clouds and flowing water essential for agriculture.

Quetzalcóatl is the name of an ancient Mesoamerican god and also of a priest-king who ruled the Toltecs in the tenth century. The glamour of the god rubbed off on the king until their legends became entwined. As god or king or both, Quetzalcóatl was credited in later days with the arts of civilization, such as calendar reckoning, rituals, music, herb medicine, and gold casting. He had even turned himself into an ant to bring man the gift of corn from the earth's recesses. But the Quetzalcóatl who was the Toltecs' king was human enough to let enemies tempt him with pulque brewed from the century plant. He woke with a hangover and a sense of remorse that drove him to abandon his palaces and march to the Gulf, where he cast himself, it was said, onto a funeral pyre and his heart rose from the purifying flames as the planet Venus.

Quetzalcóatl's story carries more than a hint of troubled times, yet the Toltecs created a civilization centered on Tula, just north of the Valley of Mexico, that left its mark on places as far away as Yucatán and New Mexico.

The Aztecs, who spoke much the same language as the Toltecs and were perhaps their poor relatives, looked back on these times as a golden age and attributed to their predecessors some of the glories of Teotihuacán's even earlier civilization. Teotihuacán, in the northeast of the Valley of Mexico, overlapped in time with ancient Rome and was a great city before London existed. Its massive sun and moon pyramids were raised toward the beginning of the Christian era and were followed by works of art like the Temple of Quetzalcóatl and palace murals praising the bounty of the rain god Tláloc. A legend of later times places the birth of the present sun in Teotihuacán. Ours is the Fifth Sun, *el Quinto Sol,* the others having disappeared in catastrophes in which lower forms of men were destroyed by jaguars, hurricanes, hot lava, and floods, as depicted on the Aztec Calendar Stone. Teotihuacán's worldly grandeur came from the trade in obsidian, a black volcanic glass of utmost importance for making sharp tools.

Teotihuacán conducted a busy commerce with the Guatemala borderlands, where Maya priest-astronomers in vaulted temples mapped the heavens, measured the year with unequaled precision, and did their arithmetic faster than the Romans. A Maya monument bears a date corresponding to A.D. 292, but numbers and writing were known in Mesoamerica long before that. Glyphs and calendar signs were being carved at Monte Albán in Oaxaca six centuries before Christ. Olmec ceremonial centers flourished in the lower Gulf coastlands between 1200 and 800 B.C. The Olmecs were master sculptors, known alike for colossal stone heads and delicate jade work featuring jaguar-faced men who may be ancestors of later rain gods.

Behind these developments, and making them possible by freeing hands from toil in the fields, was the steady improvement of corn and other food crops over thousands of years. And behind the Chicanos of today are all the civilizations that rose in Mexico, bestowing on them a spiritual heritage unsurpassed in depth and feeling by the different richness flowing from Spain.

CHAPTER 17

PAINFUL BIRTH

THE Spanish Conquest was a triumph of steel over stone. The invaders came dressed in iron, riding "deer as tall as housetops," in an Aztec chronicler's words. Their guns resounded like thunder; their swords didn't crumble like obsidian; and the iron bolts from their crossbows went humming and zinging through human flesh.

It was widely assumed then, and is still, that the Spaniards were much more "advanced" than the Indians. Spain was the heir to Mediterranean and Middle Eastern civilizations and had recently learned to print books and cross the Atlantic. Nevertheless, the Aztecs were not easy to write off. Two centuries ago the Jesuit historian Francisco Javier Clavijero, whose *Ancient History of Mexico* is still read and admired, wrote that the Spaniards found a much higher state of culture in Mexico than the Romans did when they came to Spain.

Modern scholars frequently compare pre-Spanish Mexico with Egypt and Babylonia of Bible times, which seems fair enough if technology is the yardstick. But if civilization means more than that, perhaps Tenochtitlan is entitled to some Brownie points. It was probably cleaner than any city in the world today. Doors were never locked, robberies almost unknown. The law courts, Spanish sources agree, were incorruptible. The well-dressed man carried flowers; they were part of a warrior's dress uniform. Education was free and universal. Homeless children were unknown. The *capulli,* a barrio organization of neighbors and kin, took care of orphans and the poor and aged.

If Spain brought Mexico useful plants, Mexico gave the world tomatoes, avocados, chocolate, vanilla, chicle, rubber, beans of many kinds, and most of the cotton we use today. Mexico's corn, along with Peru's potatoes and Old World wheat and rice, are the world's leading food crops. However, Mexico lacked domestic animals larger than dogs and turkeys, a handicap that slowed material development, including mobile warfare.

The defense of Mexico against Spanish steel and cavalry was led in the final desperate months by Cuauhtémoc, the last Aztec king. Barely twenty and still revered as *Joven Abuelo,* Young Grandfather, he faced up to unprecedented dangers. Past encounters among Indians had been short pitched battles. Cuauhtémoc laid in stores and weapons for a long war. He sought reconciliation with former enemies and, when this proved impossible and the city was encircled by superior numbers, he held out for an incredible ninety days. The conquistadors advanced by demolishing houses and filling the canals, but at night the Aztecs reopened them by

removing the rubble. When the city lay destroyed and fa-
mished survivors were knee-deep in the lake, lifting their
children to their shoulders, only then was Cuauhtémoc taken.

The Young Grandfather was tortured to reveal where the
Aztecs' gold was hidden. His feet were rubbed with oil and
held over burning coals, but he wouldn't talk. Eventually he
was hanged, far away from his people. By his sacrifice he left
them their dignity, and nowadays Mexicans say, "Like
Cuauhtémoc, when I am suffering, rather than give in, I endure and I laugh" (*Como Cuauhtémoc, cuando estoy sufriendo—y
antes que rajarme—me aguanto y me río*). To the poet Ramón
López Velarde, Cuauhtémoc was the "only hero who rises to
the level of art" (*único héroe a la altura del arte*). He led the
first sustained resistance of a native people to European colonization and is revered as a symbol of Mexican nationality.
The highways of the Republic are measured in kilometers
from his monument in Mexico City. There is no monument
for Cortés.

Where Cuauhtémoc made his last stand, a plaque describes
the heroic resistance as "the painful birth of the Mestizo people, who are the Mexico of today." The pain did not end
with the Conquest. So many conquistadors likened the Indians to animals, and treated them accordingly, that in 1537
Pope Paul III declared the New World peoples to be "truly
men" and capable of receiving the Christian faith. Franciscan
missionaries meanwhile had seen for themselves what their
converts could do. Indians sang in choirs and, though here-
tofore unacquainted with stringed instruments, learned so

easily to play them that their teachers were amazed.

Whatever the Indians did willingly they did well. Only a few years after the Conquest, Aztec chroniclers were writing eyewitness accounts of it in their own language, using the Spanish alphabet. No one can explain how they learned their letters, for missionary schools didn't yet exist. El Colegio de Santa Cruz de Tlatelolco dates from 1536 and is an early example of bilingual education—or rather trilingual, for the teaching was in Aztec, Spanish, and Latin. The Franciscan faculty taught philosophy, logic, arithmetic, music, and grammar, and their Indian pupils were high achievers by anyone's standards. A group of advanced students collaborated with their Latin professor, Fray Bernardino de Sahagún, in gathering a treasure-trove of information about old times, and to them we owe a large part of what we know of pre-Spanish Mexico. One large section is about Aztec medicine, which seems to have compared favorably with its sixteenth-century European counterpart. Some Spaniards, Cortés among them, consulted Aztec doctors in preference to their own.

Initially a few educated Indians, at home in two worlds, were useful in administering the colony. But after many Spaniards came clamoring for jobs, the viceroy's counselor declared that teaching Indians to read and write was "as harmful as the Devil" (*muy dañoso como el diablo*). His concern was like that of the school board chairman who asked, four hundred years later, "If we educate the Mexicans away from their work, who will transplant the onions?"

In old age, Father Sahagún saw his once-promising school falling into decay. No eager young scholars came now to bridge the plural cultures of the land. The Aztec lifeway had been based on rigor and austerity that could not be maintained after the Indians were robbed of their self-respect. It had been a mistake, the aging friar realized, to reject the Indians' ways and try to make them live as in Spain. As Sahagún wrote these melancholy lines, an epidemic was sweeping through the demoralized college. In all of Mexico it claimed a million lives, raised doubts that the Indians could survive, and led to the importation of African slaves.

The Indians did survive, though it wasn't certain they would until about 1650. From Indian villages have come many of Mexico's illustrious sons, including Benito Juárez, who preserved his country's independence in the 1860s, and Emiliano Zapata, who made the restoration of land to him who works it the burning issue of the 1910 Revolution. Many Indians, as we know, moved on to the Bajío and the North, where they linked their destiny with others in a Mestizo culture. And some went even farther north, returning as Chicanos to an ancient land of Uto-Aztecan speech, which they call Aztlán.

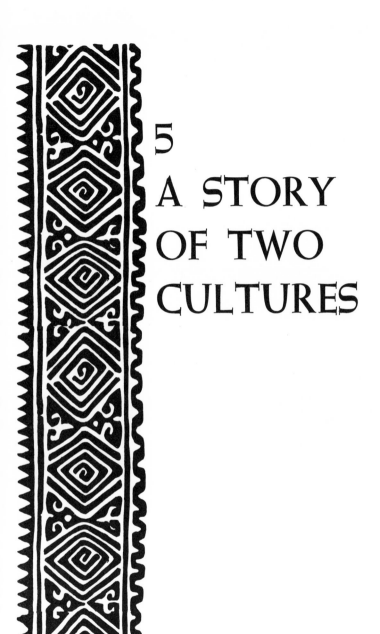

5
A STORY
OF TWO
CULTURES

CHAPTER 18

AMERICA'S MOTHER CULTURES

I F George Washington's my father, why wasn't he Chicano?" the poet Richard Olivas asked himself while attending San Jose State College. When Washington was leading thirteen Atlantic seaboard colonies to independence, Miguel Hidalgo was a young seminarian in Mexico. Taking holy orders, he became a country priest in Guanajuato, from which so many Chicanos have come. There he taught trades to his poor parishioners, started cooperative workshops, and in 1810 raised the cry of independence. He is revered as the Father of His Country in Mexico, of which California and all the Southwest were then a part. Is Father Hidalgo to be forgotten and only Washington remembered?

Countries have mothers as well as fathers. To Anglos, England is the mother country: what does "Anglo" mean if not English? Tom Paine, the pamphleteer of the American Revolution, wrote, "Europe, not England, is America's mother country." He had in mind the Irish, Scottish, German,

Dutch, and French immigrants he saw about him and many other Europeans who would be coming. England, though not their mother, proved to be a stepmother and an exacting one. If newcomers did not take to Anglo ways, their children did—and felt ashamed of their parents. Heavy nineteenth-century immigration stepped up pressure for "Americanization." America was called a melting pot. It was only patriotic for the foreign-born to submerge themselves, get rid of their peculiarities, and come out ready to be poured into a standard mold. Today, somewhat more tolerant, we have come to appreciate our Pennsylvania Dutch country, Little Italies, and Chinatowns. They are the raisins in our Anglo-Saxon pudding.

We continue, however, to think of United States history as thirteen colonies reaching out over the continent, forgetting that another and older part of our country was spreading north from Mexico. For many American citizens the mother country is Mexico, or Spain, or the Ancient America of many tribes and nations. Why don't they do like the Swedes or Poles and become Anglos after a generation or two?

One reason is that Mexican Americans have not put an ocean between themselves and the old country. Some never came to the United States: the United States came to them. For many, the crossing of a political border does not bring about much change in their life styles and associations. Those who do lose touch with their culture are more than replaced by the newly arrived. As a Chicano homeland, Aztlán is constantly reinforced from Mexico and backed up by related

Indo-Latin cultures that reach all the way to Cape Horn.

In this connection, it should be realized that prejudice closes many doors to people who don't look like Anglos. And most Chicanos, as playwright Luis Valdez has pointed out, are not "European" in their eyes, nose, skin color, and hair texture. Such physical characteristics, as anthropologists often remind us, have no known connection with innate mental ability or temperament. But our national past of African slavery, Indian wars, and border troubles has left too many Americans with "hang-ups" not easily overcome. More than one Mexican American, after trying the assimilation road, has recorded the loneliness of losing old friends without finding Anglo friends.

So the Chicanos continue to cherish their culture and its values and to reject the melting pot. This is not necessarily a case of "sour grapes." The United States is big enough for various cultures, and they have much to learn from one another. Frank S. Lopez of Los Angeles likens the melting pot theory to a jumbling of foods, saying, "If you were to mix your soup, ice cream, and entree into one pot, you would lose the taste that is inherent and pleasurable from each of the dishes that you have combined."

The playwright Valdez declares more bluntly, "Chicanos don't melt." Back of this defiant note is a conflict of cultures even older than the United States. Its highlights will help explain how differences came about and why Chicano culture is here to stay and deserves respect and appreciation.

CHAPTER 19

WHEN BRITAIN WAS UNDERDEVELOPED

THE Anglos were not always sitting on top of the world. In the fifth century, backward Germanic tribes known as Angles and Saxons came plundering the British coast and finally moved in. Spain was then suffering an incursion of Visigoths, though they had a veneer of Roman culture. No one in Europe knew of Teotihuacán in the Valley of Mexico, though it was then one of the world's largest cities.

Agriculture in Mexico dates, as we know, from about 6000 B.C. It began, so far as we know, some thousand years later in Spain and three thousand years later in Britain, which then and long after was an underdeveloped island on the rim of the world. What impetus for change there was in those early times came mostly from the Spanish peninsula. Iberians colonized both coasts of the Irish Sea two or three millennia before Christ, raising tall stone pillars and building collective tombs. They were small, dark men, the kind whose descendants in Ireland, Wales, and western England are nicknamed "Blackie." Later came the Beaker People, descendants or pupils of metallurgists who had perfected their art in Spain and carried it afar. While prospecting for tin and copper, they taught the Britons the wonder of metal tools. Still later, Cornish tin found its way through Spanish middlemen, including Greek and Carthaginian merchants established along the coast, to the bronze foundries of the Middle East.

A few centuries before Christ, warriors with iron swords, speaking Celtic tongues, swept over western Europe. Invading Spain and later Britain, they became an important element in the population of both lands. The Spaniards and the English have so many ancestors in common that plainly the differences they've had come from something other than blood. They also shared the experience of a Roman occupation, which, however, affected Spain in language and culture far more than it did Britain.

To move on to the Anglo-Saxons, they were no sooner Christianized than their northern kinsmen—warlike ancestors of today's peace-loving Scandinavians—came in waves, pillaging and settling. The last of them were William the Conqueror's Normans, civilized enough now to speak bad French. They spread a layer of their speech over an Anglo-Saxon core and thus began the English language.

Spain had new invaders in the Moors. They were North African Berbers, with a sprinkling of Syrians, Persians, and Arabs, all of whom must figure in the Chicano blood line, for they stayed eight hundred years. The Moors' final defeat came

in 1492, just before Columbus went looking in the Caribbean for China. This long period of religious strife had bright
interludes. During the centuries around the year 1000,
Spain's Moslems led Europe in culture. Students from many
lands, including England, went to Córdoba to study medicine, astronomy, and the Greek philosophers. They came
back with glowing accounts of paved streets and piped water,
fountains and orchards, silks and tapestries, Arabic numerals
that made sums simple, and paper, so much easier to write
on than parchment.

By the thirteenth century most of Spain was again under
Christian control. Fernando III of Castile, seeking reconciliation with Moslems and friendship with Jews, called himself
"king of the three religions." His son Alfonso was called "the
Wise" for his laws and his poetry. Castile had a Cortes or
parliament before England did, and Spanish towns enjoyed
rights of self-government.

Meanwhile mapmakers, in the words of the English historian Trevelyan, "placed our island on the northwest edge of
all things." England entered the sixteenth century with three
million people. Spain had eight million, besides New World
claims past imagining. If Catalina (Catherine of Aragon) was
allowed to wed Henry VIII, it was because even little England was a makeweight against big France, a neighbor and
rival of both countries.

Catalina's parents, Fernando and Isabel, had pieced
together a unified Spain from several picture-puzzle king-
doms. They'd had it out with defiant nobles who learned the

hard way that a castle can't stand up to siege guns. They restricted local liberties and surrounded themselves with a bureaucracy of lawyers and clerics whose careers depended on kingly favor. Unlike their thirteenth-century predecessors, but like most monarchs of their time, they believed that national unity required subjects to accept their rulers' faith. They were the Catholic Kings, *los Reyes Católicos,* and they made non-Christians convert or leave Spain. Many did leave, and those who remained were always suspect.

Now it happened that in large measure the Jews and Moors were Spain's physicians, merchants, financiers, truck gardeners, and skilled craftsmen. They were not easily replaced by Christians, who looked for careers to *iglesia, mar, o casa real* (Church, sea, or royal palace). If these traditional callings failed, they could go to the New World. As a result, commerce and industry were slow to develop. Place and honor belonged to the landed interests and the military and religious orders that ran sheep on lands retaken from the Moors. In the year Cortés set out to conquer Mexico, Charles I of Spain was elected emperor of the Hapsburg domains in Germany, Italy, and the Netherlands. Spain then became and long remained a piece on the chessboard of European power politics.

It was soon apparent that Spain and England had different destinies and were often to be in conflict. From the fateful sixteenth century come memories, prejudices, tastes, and beliefs that even today color the images that Anglos and Hispanos have of each other.

Some people imagine that the trouble started because
Henry VIII divorced his Spanish queen to marry Anne Bo-
leyn. It's true that he preferred the high-spirited Anne to the
pious Catalina, who wore a religious habit under her royal
robes and was as nearly a nun as a married woman can be.
She was also the aunt of the Emperor Charles and, now that
Spain belonged to the formidable Hapsburg establishment,
Henry was making friends with France. He went to great
lengths to dissolve the marriage, breaking with the Pope and
making himself head of the Church of England. Anne Bo-
leyn, whom the Spaniards called Nabolena and considered the
wickedest woman in the world, was a disappointment to
Henry. She never gave him the male heir he wanted—only
Elizabeth—and this may be one of the reasons he had her
beheaded.

A contest between England and Spain, lasting centuries,
took on the color of a religious dispute but it was that and
much more. Where Spain had sent away her foreign artisans,
England opened the door to needed skills. Where Spain sold
wool, the English sold fine woolen cloth. Elizabeth com-
manded her subjects to eat fish on both Friday and Wednes-
day but not as a religious observance. The purpose was to
build up the fishing fleet and prepare seamen for the British
Navy. Good Queen Bess lived to wear silk stockings and lace
of English make and to see blast furnaces and powder mills
rising. The diamonds and emeralds in her crown were a gift
from Francis Drake. She knighted him not so much for these
souvenirs of his American travels as for the shiploads of silver

bullion that enriched his backers, including herself. El Draque was not a pirate in English eyes but a proper Protestant who read aloud from the Book of Common Prayer before plundering a Spanish settlement.

Successive generations of English and Spanish children were now brought up to abhor each other's faith. In Britain the Inquisition and the wrongs done the Indians became the ingredients of a black legend of Spanish cruelty that was carried to the English colonies in America and on eventually to Texas and California. As if persecution and conquest were not always cruel!

When Spain's Invincible Armada sailed against England in 1588 and proved vincible, Englishmen attributed the outcome to divine favor, saying, "He blew and they were scattered." But seamanship and gunnery as well as storms had a part in the victory. The slender, easy-to-turn English vessels outsailed the enemy and delivered their broadsides from a distance. The troops the Armada carried, admittedly the best in Europe, were denied a chance to grapple, board, and close man to man. It was unchivalrous.

Miguel Cervantes, who had collected provisions for the Armada, wrote an obituary for the age of chivalry. It related the misadventures of Don Quijote, who went about to right wrongs, succor widows, and protect damsels in a world that had changed. Though sorcerers spoiled the outcome, at least they could not prevent the effort.

Spain did not collapse with the Invincible Armada but continued the effort, modernizing her Navy, drawing trea-

sure from America, and creating masterpieces of art and literature. But England failed to respect the "keep off" signs
Spain put up in the New World and instead plundered the
colonies and preyed on convoys bound for Seville. "The grain
the Spaniard sowed, the English reaped," observed the dramatist Lope de Vega. Later the intruders turned from piracy
to contraband trade, with the result that the Spanish Americans at least received good English cloth for their silver.
Eventually Spain had to look in foreign markets for goods
with which to supply her colonies. In these ways the treasure
of the Chicanos' Aztec and Spanish ancestors slipped from
Spain's hands to enrich England and the north of Europe.

Spain gave her language and culture to what are now eighteen American republics but overextended herself in an effort
to keep her colonies unchanged after three hundred years.
When at last they broke away, the territorial gap between
Spanish-speaking and English-speaking America was closing
in the Southwest. The two cultures, so long at odds on the
seas, were on the eve of a fateful rendezvous by land.

CHAPTER 20

FROM PYGMY
TO GIANT

IN 1783, when England recognized the independence of the
United States, Count Aranda of Spain felt misgivings. "The
North American nation is now a pygmy," he told his king,
"but some day it could become a giant that would threaten
the Spanish dominions in America."

"Some day" can be a long time. Right then Charles III was
concerned with protecting his flank from the British in Canada and saw no harm in letting a few Anglo-American fron-
tiersmen settle in Louisiana. They came in unexpected numbers, to the consternation of the Bishop of Louisiana, who
called them "a gang of adventurers who have no religion and
acknowledge no God." They may have called themselves
Protestants but, no matter, there was no stopping them. In
1803, when Louisiana became part of the United States, an
Anglo vanguard was already moving into Texas to hunt wild
horses and deal in contraband. Mexico's independence struggle drew in more of them. Joining irregular bands, they

fought for adventure and the hope of land, even for high ideals.

After the war, Mexico let Stephen F. Austin bring colonists into Texas, provided they were Catholics desirous of Mexican citizenship. Considering how frontier Anglos were raised to hate the Pope and everything Spanish, it was astonishing how many overcame their prejudices and took title to 640 acres of good farm land. Soon other colonies were springing up, with or without permission.

Newly independent Mexico, exhausted by war and beset with problems, exercised little control over distant Texas. However, in 1828 General Manuel de Mier y Terán was sent there to investigate. He reported that many of the Anglo-Americans he met were either ex-convicts with branded cheeks or men of substance who had come with their slaves to grow cotton. Slavery had been abolished in Mexico, but the settlers had little patience with Mexican laws and officials, though some, like Austin, tried to wrestle with unfamiliar red tape. What a pity the Comanches stole his Spanish grammar! Many of his countrymen saw no sense in waiting weeks for supplies from Saltillo or Mexico City when they could buy from New Orleans, and cheaper too, if only they were excused from paying customs duties.

Two lifeways were already in conflict. Anglos who had been taught that the only good Indian was a dead Indian were not disposed to kowtow to Mexicans, who to their mind were little, if any, better than Indians. General Terán saw all this and warned his government, "If timely measures are not taken, Texas will sink the country." Feeble efforts were made to halt the Anglo inflow. It was too late; already they outnumbered the Texas Mexicans. Mexico itself was in turmoil, trying to cast off colonial abuses but sliding toward military rule.

Everyone knows how General Santa Anna marched against Texas and reduced the Alamo in blood and fire. Yet few are aware that a number of Mexicans died in the Alamo, fighting against Santa Anna under the Mexican flag. Or that Juan Seguín raised a company of San Antonio Mexicans who served with Sam Houston at San Jacinto. These Texas Mexicans who took up arms against Santa Anna's tyranny were placed in the difficult position of making common cause with the Anglo-Texans. Some, like Seguín, lived to regret their choice. He became mayor of San Antonio but never stood in well with the Anglos. Tiring after ten years of racial slurs, he went to live in Mexico. In 1974 it was the Texans' turn to have regrets, and they brought his body from Nuevo Laredo and buried it with honors in Seguin, Texas.

If the English were proud of being Anglo-Saxons, the Yankees were more so, and the Texans most of all. There was much talk in the early days of Anglo-Saxon America's "manifest destiny to overspread the continent." Texans expected no small part in the enterprise. In 1841, six military companies set out from San Antonio with proclamations inviting the New Mexicans to become "members of our young Republic." They lost their way, fell prisoner, and were sent by forced marches to Mexico City. En route the captured soldiers were treated sometimes harshly, sometimes with kindness. After a few months' imprisonment, they were released. One of them wrote an angry book about their hardships. Now forgotten except in Texas, it inflamed anti-Mexican sentiment anew. What rankled most in Texan hearts was not so much the rigors of a long journey as the indignity of being prisoners of Mexicans, a despised people at once Catholic, Spanish, and Indian.

Mexicans were not easy for Anglos to understand. United States President James K. Polk, writing in his diary in 1846, called them "that stubborn and impracticable people." After losing Texas, they had turned down a good cash offer for California and New Mexico. And now, after a clash on the Rio Grande, the two countries were at war. The war was more popular in the South than in the North. Congressman Abraham Lincoln of Illinois raised his voice against it. Henry Thoreau of Massachusetts passed a night in jail rather than pay taxes to a government which he felt was fighting to extend slavery. The experience led him to write an essay on civil disobedience which, in later times, deeply influenced Mahatma Gandhi and Martin Luther King, Jr.

Nevertheless, a poor opinion of Mexico and the Mexicans was so widespread that General Stephen W. Kearny, upon occupying New Mexico, told the people, "We come among you for your benefit, not for your injury." The Mexican governor Juan Bautista Vigil replied tactfully, "Do not find it strange if there is no manifestation of joy and enthusiasm." He added that Mexico, for all her misfortunes, "was our mother" and asked, "What child will not shed abundant tears at the tomb of his parents?"

Soon after, Susan Magoffin, the eighteen-year-old bride of a Santa Fe trader, arrived in occupied New Mexico. Her diary lends insight into Anglo attitudes. The first Mexicans she saw were "wild-looking strangers," while the women, pulling their dresses above their knees to cross a creek, caused her to draw her veil closely to "protect my blushes." Onlookers watching her carriage being repaired seemed as "void of refinement, judgement &. as the dumb animals" until one of them called her *"bonita muchachita"* (pretty little girl), whereupon she found them "a very quick and intelligent people."

Later, Susan wrote, "What a polite people these Mexicans are, altho' they are looked upon as a half barbarous set by the generality of people." Her good opinion, alas, was to be modified. Kearny's well-disciplined troops moved on to California and were replaced by an occupying force whose overbearing conduct fed resentment in people already humiliated over the lack of determined resistance to the invaders. In Taos, the American governor and a number of his friends died in an Indian and Mexican uprising. Susan, fearing the revolt might spread, concluded that among the Mexicans there were "smooth-faced assassins . . . and some good people too."

Neither in New Mexico nor California did the Spanish-speaking people have much love lost for the government at Mexico City. It changed with bewildering frequency in those chaotic days and neglected the outlying provinces or sent self-serving politicians to rule them. There was little possibility of effective resistance to the Anglos, nor much enthusiasm for undertaking it, so long as the occupying forces respected local customs. This they did not always know how to do. California was as good as conquered until an officious captain put a curfew on Los Angeles, prohibiting social gatherings and mortifying local sensibilities to the point where Mexican irregulars retook the city and held it several months. For his part, General Andrés Pico redeemed Mexican honor in a cavalry clash at San Pascual near San Diego. It put General Kearny out of action for a spell and upset the invasion timetable.

The main theater of the war was the interior of Mexico and the capital itself, which was taken after a last-ditch stand by teen-age cadets at Chapultepec Castle, who are remembered as *los Niños Héroes,* the Boy Heroes. The occupying army stayed nine months. General Winfield Scott held a tight rein on the regulars, but the volunteers, among them Indian fighters from the raw frontier, were ungovernable. Their conduct, Scott himself declared, was such as to make "every American of Christian morals blush for his country."

By the treaty of Guadalupe Hidalgo, Mexico surrendered half her territory to the United States. The pygmy, as Aranda had foreseen, was now a giant.

CHAPTER 21

CHICANO FOLK HEROES

LIVING next door to a giant is upsetting sometimes. "Poor Mexico," a Mexican President once said, "so far from God, so near the United States."

The young giant was rather given to bragging. He attributed his immense success to steady habits and could only conclude that his luckless neighbor was lazy and, for that reason, poor. From the 1840s on, it was a commonplace to say that the "degenerate Mexicans" must make way for the "more vigorous Anglo-Saxon race." Any attempt by Mexicans to prove otherwise marked them as cruel and treacherous. A whole generation of young people was brought up on dime novels in which the Anglo hero walked tall and the villain was a sneaky Mexican.

Between peoples so estranged, trouble was inevitable. The Mexicans, though weaker, had their dignity and pride. When a high-spirited Mexican felt goaded beyond endurance, he was capable of seeking retribution without counting the consequences. Then his bold deeds would come to be sung in corridos and improved on down the years.

Joaquín Murrieta rode at the head of a band of desperadoes in California in the early 1850s, robbing travelers and making war on all gringos. For in his eyes what he did was war, not banditry. Legend has it that ruffians had jumped his mining claim and murdered his wife Rosita after raping her. What is certain is that his countrymen were ousted from the diggings by a foreign miners' tax and by lynchings and armed attacks. Murrieta became a Mexican Robin Hood with a $1,000 price on his head. This seemed so paltry a sum, they say, that he changed the amount on a "wanted" poster to $10,000 and signed his name. He was everywhere at once, or so reports made it seem. After a shootout in 1853, a body was identified rightly or wrongly as his. The head, preserved in brandy, was taken on a world tour, then displayed in San Francisco until lost in the 1906 earthquake.

In New Mexico, Father Antonio José Martínez championed his people both before and after annexation, founding schools and printing textbooks. It is widely believed, though not proved, that he had a part in the Taos uprising against the Anglo-Americans. When that failed, he worked within the new order and served with distinction in the territorial assembly. Father Martínez with his "violent Spanish face" is somewhat of a villain in Willa Cather's *Death Comes for the Archbishop,* published in 1927, when melting-pot ideas held sway. Though fond of women and good living, he was deeply religious after his fashion and was held in respect by the

Penitentes. A generation had passed since the Franciscans departed. During that period the New Mexican Church had gone its own way almost unnoticed, firm in some traditional observances, lax in others.

After the Stars and Stripes were raised, Bishop Jean Batiste Lamy was sent from Cincinnati to put matters aright. He had an instant run-in with the Hispano clergy and especially with Father Martínez. Bishop Lamy, though a dedicated and able churchman, was insensitive to Hispano culture. In building schools, convents, and churches, including the Cathedral at Santa Fe, he ignored Spanish and Pueblo traditional styles. Believing that New Mexicans, as United States citizens, should put their Hispanic past behind them, he tried to suppress the Penitentes but only drove them underground. And though he excommunicated Father Martínez, the disobedient priest held the loyalty of his Taos parishioners while he lived.

In 1947 a successor of Archbishop Lamy restored the blessing of the Church to the Penitentes, recommending only that they practice moderation in their penances. Father Martínez is no longer a Willa Cather villain but a Chicano hero. He combined liberal educational and political principles with respect for old-fashioned religious practices. The common denominator of this seeming paradox was his unshakable belief in the right of his people to choose their own way of life.

To be a hero in the Texas borderlands in the nineteenth century called for someone like heavy-set, red-bearded Cheno Cortina. Cheno (short for Juan Nepomuceno) was descended from the first cattleman to settle north of the Rio Grande. And he was kin to about all the Tejanos in the lower Valley; his mother's family had a land grant claim to the site where Brownsville stands. There were too many Texas Mexicans around Brownsville for the Anglo-Texans to order them out on three days' notice, as was happening in some counties to the north. Instead, a running battle over land titles went on, sometimes with arms but more often in the courts. It was consuming the fortunes of the Tejanos in lawyers' fees, whether they won or lost.

The flash point was near. In 1859 the Cortina War started over a cup of coffee in a Brownsville cafe. Cheno had been a young cavalryman during the war which Mexicans call the North American Intervention. He was now a cattleman of thirty-five. On July 13 he rode into town with his vaqueros for a morning snack. Over his coffee he saw the city marshal manhandling a tipsy prisoner who was an old family servant of the Cortinas. "Take it easy," said Cheno. The peace officer cursed him and received back a shot in the shoulder. Cheno rescued the prisoner and rode off. The deed made him a Tejano hero, but he knew he was a marked man.

Up and down the river went Cortina, recruiting guerrillas. In the fall, he rode into Brownsville at the head of his men and temporarily occupied the city. He issued a proclamation breathing defiance to crooked lawyers and vowing that "our personal enemies shall not possess our land until they have fattened it with their own gore." Cheno's raiders looted ranches, ran off cattle, tangled with volunteers and regulars, and made attacks upriver as far as Rio Grande City. The concerted efforts of Texas Rangers and Robert E. Lee's army command drove them into Mexico, but forays into Texas continued.

During the American Civil War, which coincided with the French Intervention in Mexico, Cortina became a patriot hero. Juárez named him governor of Tamaulipas, and he cooperated with United States Union forces. At one time he was simultaneously fighting to keep the French out of Matamoros and the Confederates out of Brownsville. After the war he was military commander of his state. Union sympathies had not increased his popularity among the Texans, and he was blamed for continuing lawlessness along the border, though a postwar crop of badmen of both nations had a large part in it. In 1875, to ease tensions, General Cortina was retired to Mexico City, where he faded away, as old soldiers do.

The Cortina War was only one phase of a struggle that rocked South Texas for nearly a century and sometimes took on the proportions of a border war. It was marked by shootings, lynchings, robberies, border crossings in both directions to steal cattle or take vengeance, and hundreds of encounters never recorded and now forgotten. The violence which began in the 1830s subsided somewhat after the 1870s but flared anew during the Pancho Villa and German spy scares of World War I and the influx of refugees from the Mexican Revolution.

The Texas Mexicans and the tan-clad Texas Rangers in

their wide-brimmed hats became hereditary enemies, passing their animosities from father to son. *Los rinches,* as the Rangers were called, were reputed to "shoot first and investigate afterwards" where Mexicans were concerned, and stories went around of Rangers who boasted they'd killed a certain number of men, "not counting Mexicans." To stand up to the rinches was the supreme test of valor, celebrated in corridos. They still sing of Jacinto Treviño of Matamoros, whose brother was beaten to death in Brownsville. Jacinto avenges the crime and bears his brother's body home. The rinches put a price on his head. Jacinto returns to Brownsville, shoots it out with them, killing several, and goes back over the river. Is it truth, fantasy, or something of both? *¿Quién sabe?* Who knows? It is a heroic narrative of a people's memories of an earlier day.

This deeply rooted culture conflict is far from resolved, and the Texas Chicanos still lag behind those of other states in schooling, job opportunities, and other indicators of well-being. But a young generation is looking to the future. More and more Texas colleges offer Chicano studies. In the winter of 1969–70 a group of young Chicanos were harvesting carrots in the Lower Rio Grande Valley. Some were dropouts and some, having been discouraged from continuing in school, said they were pushouts. All had come to realize the importance of passing a high school equivalency examination and were studying together after work in an abandoned monastery. Out of their efforts a college developed, a Chicano college. It moved into an old mansion in Mercedes, Texas, and, besides preparatory work, now offers undergraduate courses and a master's degree program for prospective teachers. Graduates and undergraduates receive credit from Antioch College of Ohio. The school has close ties with the Valley *campesinos* or farm workers, and it enrolls many of their sons and daughters, preparing them to help their community. The name of the school is Colegio Jacinto Treviño.

 CHAPTER 22

MOTHER EARTH'S ORPHANS

WHEN the Treaty of Guadalupe Hidalgo, ending the war with Mexico, was drafted in 1848, the Mexican representatives tried to do what they could for their countrymen who would henceforth live in the United States. That is why the treaty promises that Mexicans in the ceded territories will be "protected in the free enjoyment of their liberty and property."

"Without these rights," said a Mexican negotiator, "our brothers will become strangers in their own land."

Chicanos complain, like their parents and grandparents before them, that these rights have been poorly respected and that they are indeed strangers in their own land. To understand how they feel it is necessary to review some unhappy episodes.

Their property was the good earth. In the Rio Arriba country, people say, "The land is our mother. If we lose the land we are orphans. Where will we go?"

The California rancheros never imagined in the 1840s that they might lose their land. Eight hundred families held the great ranchos. The few Yankees were lucky to break into society—like Abel Stearns, who had married one of the Bandini girls and was now Don Abel. That was in southern California. Up north, Mariano Vallejo was one of several *influyentes* (influential men) who wearied of Mexico's unending troubles and were half-reconciled to California's becoming one of the United States—as it did.

Had there been no gold rush, the rancheros' gracious way of life might have lasted a while. But a hundred thousand treasure hunters flocked into California, and only a few struck it rich. The rest, unless they went home, looked for a place to settle. Some were veterans of the war with Mexico. They cast envious eyes on the ranchos and asked themselves why so much land should belong to people they had defeated in battle. Not many of them knew what was in the Treaty of Guadalupe Hidalgo—and not all of them would have cared.

The fate of the rancheros was sealed in 1851, when the new state of California persuaded Congress to set up a board of land commissioners to decide which Spanish and Mexican land titles were good and which were not. The commissioners tried to be fair but were handicapped by their ignorance of Mexican law and the Spanish language. Seeing the problem through Anglo eyes, they asked for written titles and surveys naming exact boundaries. Now a ranchero could bring in witnesses of good repute to testify that it was common knowledge that the land in question was his. But how could he produce a document that, if it existed at all, might date from a time when no surveyors were to be had and the boundaries were an ancient cow path, a tree long since dead, and the horizon seen from a certain hilltop? Hearings and appeals went on for years. More often than not, for a wonder, the ranchero's title was finally validated. But by then he was deep in debt and might owe half his land to his Anglo lawyer. Worse yet, squatters had by now moved onto his rancho, putting up fences and other "improvements" on what they claimed was "unoccupied land." They were not easily dislodged, for some had trigger-happy fingers and all of them had votes to offer politicians willing to champion their cause.

Thus in California, as in Texas, the grants of Spanish kings and Mexican governors were steadily eroded. Tax bills were sent out now, not on the yield of the land as in former times, but on the land itself, whether cultivated or not. If a ranchero neglected to pay, having less money than cattle or not reading English, a stranger would buy the property at a tax sale and perhaps sell it back to him—but of course at a profit. Next time the forewarned ranchero would borrow money at high interest to pay his taxes, risking foreclosure. Don Pío Pico, governor of California before the takeover, had been generous, perhaps too generous, with land grants to his friends, but during the drought of the 1860s in the cow counties he fell deep in debt to Don Abel Stearns and others and was reduced to poverty, like his brother Andrés. The popular Picos had many compadres who had co-signed their notes, and they too were ruined.

In his old age, Mariano Vallejo, who had once admired the Anglos, wrote that it was natural for individuals to seek their own good "but I denounce it on the part of a government that promised to respect our rights and to treat us as its own sons."

Not until 1884 did anyone speak up for the vanishing Californios and find listeners. In that year appeared Helen Hunt Jackson's *Ramona,* a sympathetic if romantic story of rancho life and an indictment of continuing injustices against California's Mexicanized Indians. Two generations read the book, weeping. There are still aging Ramonas all over California, named for the heroine.

New Mexico presents a similar story of title hearings, tax sales, and foreclosures. But Hispano roots were deeper than in California, and community feeling was stronger, especially in the northern villages. The people, linked by ancestral blood ties and communal traditions, continued to fight for the free enjoyment of their property. Only it was a kind of property that the latecoming Anglos did not understand or care for.

The land in question was held by descendants of the first settlers. Sometimes they helped one another with clearing, planting, and harvesting; sometimes they preferred to work their strips of land alone. But in either case the surrounding *ejido,* or commons, was open to all. There the villagers pastured their animals, hunted, fished, and gathered firewood. It is often written that Spanish colonists lacked experience in local self-government, but here on the northern borderlands the villagers had their *ayuntamiento,* as democratic as a New

England town meeting, and their good faith in handling water rights, for example, has been mentioned.

The surveyor-general, who came representing the United States, did not know what to make of all this. He believed that the commons, unless clearly bounded, ought to be state or federal land and, in any case, must be properly taxed. This was bad news to the villagers, who lived by barter and hardly saw a dollar from one month to another. To the Anglos even a farm was "unoccupied land" unless there was a house on it. Didn't they know that Hispanos live in villages and go out to the fields to work? Then land speculators came and tried to break up the communal pattern. By buying out some needy heir, a speculator could sue for a division of the property or else graze a huge herd on the commons to the distress of his neighbors. "This man does not look on the ejido with raza eyes or a raza heart," they'd say.

Around 1870, the territorial governor sold most of the Spanish-Mexican land records for waste paper or threw them away. More were destroyed in a capitol fire in 1892. These were the years of the Santa Fe Ring, a combination of Anglo politicians and speculators and rich Spanish Americans who diverted millions of acres into their own hands. They were also the years when Texas cattlemen and Hispano sheepmen were shooting it out and the Gorras Blancas were cutting wire. The government dissolved the local ayuntamientos, and much of the common land they had administered went to the railroad builders and later into national forests. By the century's end, all but a few of the village land claims had been disallowed.

The present century saw the coming of drainage projects and huge dams that were a boon to commercial farming but ruined Hispano farmers too poor to pay assessments. The Forest Service, which at first had not interfered with villagers who grazed a few animals in the forests, now began acquiring more ejido land and laying down rules. Forestry officials are charged with conserving and putting to good use a valuable natural resource, but in the Taos and Rio Arriba country they did not look on their mission with a raza heart. Seeing the region's great recreational possibilities, they kept cutting down on grazing permits until the villagers could no longer make a living and half of them were on welfare.

"They take away our land and give us powdered milk," grumbled the villagers, watching the vacationers' cars rolling by with guns, fishing rods, and yapping dogs.

By grazing a cow on land they'd used since the seventeenth century, a family could supply its own milk. True, the Forest Service said the land was hurt from overgrazing. But who was causing the damage? The Hispano with his family herd? Or the big stockmen and the commercial logging operators who left the hillsides gullied?

Some forestry officials were saying privately that there was no future for these small farmers, and the sooner they went to Albuquerque or Los Angeles the better. Two lifeways were in confrontation.

Out of these clashing attitudes came the Land Grant War of 1967. It was like the Gorras Blancas riding again, but this time their leader was Reies Tijerina and his strategy was to deny with dramatic deeds that the Anglos' law was law at all.

Tijerina has been called a saint, a fanatic, and a devil. He was born into a large family of Texas migrants and grew up during the Great Depression, raiding garbage cans, missing school, and always moving. His religious mother, while she lived, told him the meek would inherit the earth, while the talk of his father's people was of the miseries they would meanwhile undergo. By family tradition they were the rightful heirs of a Laredo land grant of which they had been robbed. Grandfather sometimes told how he was strung up by vigilantes and only cut down when a passerby said, "He's not the one." No wonder the child had nightmares. But he also had a dream that was almost a vision of heaven's green pastures and God choosing him to lead his people from bondage.

Reies Tijerina briefly attended a Bible school and became a wandering preacher. His travels took him into the Rio Arriba country and also to Mexico, where he delved into the colonial archives and made himself a walking encyclopedia on land grants. When about thirty-five, a solid man now with backswept jet hair, he began organizing what was to be the Alianza Federal de Pueblos Libres, the Federation of Free City-States. "City-State" was his name for the self-governing ayuntamientos the Anglo authorities had abolished in 1882.

For five years Tijerina moved through the hills, talking in adobe cottages with villagers who squatted on dirt floors. He climbed from low key to ecstasy delivering his unvarying message that the land was theirs by right. What they already believed he put into words, but the question remained of what to do. Their petitions had been ignored. Tijerina led them to the conclusion that they must hammer home untiringly to the nation and the world that the government and its agencies were in illegal possession of their lands. They must issue eviction notices to the United States, no less, and the state of New Mexico. And they must back their claims by symbolic action that could not be ignored.

In the fall of 1966, this dreamer-turned-militant led the *Aliancistas* to the old San Joaquin land grant in a national forest. They proclaimed it a "free City-State," then "arrested" two forest rangers, found them "guilty" of trespassing on the community's land, and released them unharmed.

Tijerina soon faced a series of federal charges and was under heavy bond but remained unrepentant. As his name became a byword in Rio Arriba, the Alianza scheduled a barbecue at Coyote, expecting a big turnout. The Spanish-surnamed district attorney was alarmed. At least so he said, though some of his constituents declared he was miffed at being called a *vendido,* a sellout. At any rate, he didn't wait for the barbecue but declared it in advance to be an illegal assembly and had the state police scouring the hills for Tijerina. They didn't find him, but several of his colleagues were arrested, and when people arrived for the barbecue they found the gates of the picnic site locked and the road blocked by patrol cars.

It was Tijerina's move. Two days later, on June 5, 1967, came what is remembered as the Tierra Amarilla courthouse raid. Only it wasn't a raid in Tijerina's book. It was an attempt to release the prisoners and make a citizen's arrest of the district attorney for violating their rights of peaceable assembly. If a citizen witnesses a robbery, he has a right to arrest the robber—if he can. Tijerina argued that a citizen has the same right to arrest a government official who is breaking the law.

The arresting party took the courthouse by surprise. There were twenty of them, armed with automatic rifles or at least with the guns every villager has for shooting rabbits. One man had sticks of dynamite in his belt, for district attorneys are not arrested by warrants alone. As it happened, the D.A. was not in the courthouse that day and the prisoners had just been released on bond. Nothing went as planned. A police officer who reached for his gun and was beaten to the draw was injured, as was the jailer, who tried to flee. Tijerina testified later that he did all he could to stop violence. His men left, taking two hostages, and were pursued by patrol cars, jeeps, tanks, and helicopters. They were picked up, slowly however, and meanwhile fifty supposed sympathizers, mostly old men, women, and children, were held in a sheep pen for thirty hours, refusing with Spanish pride the C-rations national guardsmen offered them.

Now at last a spotlight was on a despoiled people who were strangers in their own land. As for Tijerina, who could count all the charges, federal and state, that were pending against him? Pleading his own case before a jury, he won acquittal on some of them, but the prosecutions continued and he served prison terms totaling some two and a half years. His people, meanwhile, had an enhanced sense of pride, especially the young. They were calling for Hispano studies in the schools and were setting up health clinics and farm co-ops. They honored their teacher, who had raised *la causa,* the cause, to a level where it no longer depended solely on an inspired leader. Even the federal agencies had moved a step beyond powdered milk and were sponsoring programs to improve the quality of rural life and establish small village industries.

Will the government relent and give back much of New Mexico to the land-grant heirs? Probably not even Tijerina ever hoped for so much. But the Hispanos, or the Chicanos as many call themselves, do expect compensation for their losses and generous help to rebuild a life of their own choosing.

To show how the weak can exact a measure of justice from the strong, Tijerina has often told the story of the lion and the cricket. The lion boasted of being the king of beasts and was always insulting the cricket's pride. When the cricket could stand no more, he challenged his adversary to a fight. The lion prepared to swallow the little fellow whole, but the cricket hopped into the lion's ear and began tickling him and making him itch. The king of beasts clawed at his ear until it bled, but the cricket wouldn't stop and the lion had to give in. So the cricket won the battle, "and we," Tijerina would add, "shall do the same."

6
A PEOPLE WHOSE TIME HAS COME

 CHAPTER 23

THEY GIVE US
A HARD TIME

THE walls in Montebello and Belvedere and on North Broadway in Los Angeles have changed. Carlitos has stopped drawing arrow-pierced hearts proclaiming his love for Conchita. Instead he prints in big black letters, *"Abajo con* absentee landlords," meaning down with slumlords who charge high rents for run-down living quarters. Or perhaps his graffito has a political thrust, like *"Abajo con* gerrymandering," and is a protest against the practice of carving up the barrio so that it's hard to elect a Chicano to the city council or the state legislature.

Wall legends echo urban discontents. They sound bilingual calls to action like *"Organísense, Raza"* (Get organized, Raza) and "If not now, when?" Always a favorite is Benito Juárez's famous saying, *"El respeto al derecho ajeno es la paz"* (Respect for the rights of others in peace). Graffiti often include a "C/S," short for *Con Safos,* which, besides being the name of a lively magazine which pictures slogans like these, means lay off and let the message stay. It also means "same to you" to anyone who disagrees. It's barrio slang, like *"Nos dan mucha carria"* (They give us a hard time).

It's four to one, in the cities now, that a Chicano holds a job like handling freight, pressing pants, stoking kilns, cleaning fish, stocking supermarket shelves, or wheeling hospital patients to their X-ray appointments. One Anglo in seven has professional or technician status but only one Chicano in twelve. The latter has few chances to climb the company's executive ladder; any well-off Chicano is apt to be a doctor or a lawyer with a good practice and a lucky real estate investment. Chicano family incomes in Los Angeles average something over half those of Anglos; in San Antonio, less than half.

The first Chicano prelate in the United States was Auxiliary Bishop Patrick Flores of San Antonio. At a 1973 rally for the right of clothing, meat-packing, and machine workers to organize and bargain collectively, the bishop said, "Even with full-time work, almost half the people living on the Westside are living in poverty. San Antonio does not need alms and welfare. San Antonio needs just wages."

Everywhere in Aztlán the Chicano unemployment rate is high. It's hard to get even an unskilled job without a high school diploma. Three out of four Chicano adults do not have one. In 1970 a typical Chicano had eight years of schooling, compared to ten for Blacks and twelve for Anglos. Late in the 1960s, through the efforts of the League of United Latin American Citizens, the American G.I. Forum, and the Community Service Organization, federal funds were voted to help Chicanos overcome this deficiency and learn the skills required to be a welder, a computer technician, a medical secretary, and so on. However, projects like this have their political ups and downs. They may taper off or be turned over to local authorities who don't have the money or interest to continue them.

Even the usual public services are neglected in the barrios, as evidenced by uncollected garbage, unpaved streets, sidewalks if any in bad repair, and run-down schools and playgrounds.

Barrio health facilities are busy and crowded. Patients who are handled brusquely may suffer in silence rather than return for treatment. A Colorado study shows Chicanos living an average of ten years less than Anglos. Infant mortality is high and so is the death rate from pneumonia and tuberculosis. Chicanos who have done stoop labor tend to have painful back trouble. This is made worse by the short-handled hoe, *el cortito,* which compels a laborer to bend almost to the ground to thin and weed his row. Ten years of this will wreck a man, say Chicanos.

Suppose a Chicano couple and an Anglo couple in similar circumstances go shopping for a car or a TV set. No need to guess who is asked the higher price. Field research shows it's the Chicanos. In one case, a gas range priced at $200 in East Los Angeles was on sale in an Anglo neighborhood for $110.

Anglo youngsters are taught that "the policeman is your friend," the man who answers questions politely and holds up traffic for old ladies to cross the street. Anglos rarely see the policeman on the beat. In the barrio he's much in evidence, testing locked doors, cruising with lights flashing, even hovering over the rooftop in a helicopter. Barrio policemen are overwhelmingly Anglos. Few Chicanos are accepted for police duty, if only because of height requirements. Many a Chicano who is tall enough for infantry combat duty is too short to be a policeman. And an Anglo police force is unfortunately not free of the prejudices of the population from which it is drawn.

Chicanos, for their part, have a distrust of authority as old as the Spanish Conquest, the Texas border troubles, and Porfirio Díaz's dictatorship. A sense of dignity runs deep in their culture. If a Chicano is shoved and called names while being questioned, the stage is set for confrontation. The Chicano talks back. The police officer, feeling his authority questioned, swings with his billy club. More angry words, a charge of "resisting arrest," and a youth who may be innocent of wrongdoing has a police record that will interfere with his chances of employment and higher education.

So familiar is this pattern that the United States Commission on Civil Rights, under the chairmanship of Father Theodore M. Hesburgh of Notre Dame, conducted a study of Mexican Americans and the administration of justice in the Southwest. "Our investigations," reported the Commission, "reveal that Mexican American citizens are subject to unduly harsh treatment by law enforcement officers, that they are often arrested on insufficient grounds, receive physical and verbal abuse, and penalties which are disproportionately severe." Too often, young Chicano offenders are sent to reformatories while Anglos, in the same circumstances, are merely placed in the custody of their parents. The report condemns "stop and frisk" practices in Chicano neighborhoods, harassment by frequent automobile safety checks, and shooting to kill suspects who run.

The Commission report also deplores the near-absence of Chicanos on grand juries and trial juries. If a Chicano defendant can't raise bail, he waits in jail for his trial. If his English is poor, he may sign a confession he doesn't understand. His counsel is likely to be the public defender or a court-appointed attorney. The lawyer, a busy man, may advise his Chicano client to plead guilty and hope for a light sentence.

Such abuses call for more political muscle than Chicanos yet possess. Their voting strength has never corresponded to their numbers. Early immigrants expected to return to Mexico and considered it a rejection of their motherland to seek United States citizenship. Their children wondered whether naturalization was worthwhile "when they will still treat me as a Mexican." Today's foreign-born Chicanos know their destiny lies in the United States. Citizenship offers protection and hope of better times. Often, though, they hold back from fear. Some are "without documents," which is worse than being without a shadow. Not necessarily "illegals," they may have mislaid their papers or come as babies with parents long since called to their reward. Even those having documents may speak too little English to pass the United States history and government examination. For that matter, native-born citizens, especially from Texas, don't always have birth certificates. Or when it's time to register, they are picking cherries a thousand miles away.

Nevertheless, most present-day Chicanos are citizens by birth and hence a potential force. The Viva Kennedy clubs of 1960 swung many votes to President John F. Kennedy and tipped the balance in the crucial Illinois race. Out of that experience grew the Mexican American Political Association (MAPA) in California and the Political Association of Spanish Speaking Organizations (PASSO) in Texas. Recently some of the more militant Chicanos, soured on the "empty promises" of the major parties, have organized the La Raza Unida Party in several states. It has won local elections in South Texas and sees itself gaining the balance of power in many places.

"Community control" has recently become a byword among Chicanos. The community can be a town with a Chicano majority or an urban barrio that would like to run its own internal affairs. There are varying degrees of control.

In Los Angeles, the Community Service Organization supports self-help projects such as a buyers club, a consumer complaint center, a credit union, group insurance, death benefits, citizenship classes, voter registration drives, home ownership counseling, and protests against discrimination in employment.

The Chicano writer Armando B. Rendon suggests organizing barrio unions to bargain collectively with public authorities. If they neglect to provide street lights, sidewalks, sewers, job opportunities, and the like, the union could picket city hall and recommend withholding votes and even taxes.

The ultimate in community control would be for the institutions of the barrio to be run by the people of the barrio. The police would be drawn from the barrio itself and be familiar with its language and culture. So would the personnel of health and welfare services. Chicanos and Chicanas would be encouraged to qualify as teachers in barrio schools.

Already an East Los Angeles Community Union has taken what is regarded as a first step toward a measure of control over barrio business life. With help from foundations and unions, it is sponsoring workshops and retail outlets of which the employees and customers will be part owners. Chicanos have a long tradition of mutual help for survival through benefit societies and networks of kin. Will they now turn it to account, building cooperative enterprises of much greater scope?

 CHAPTER 24

FED UP

VARIOUS Mexican American organizations, meeting at Corpus Christi, Texas, in 1929, formed the League of United Latin American Citizens (LULAC) "to develop within the members of our race the best, purest and most perfect type of true and loyal citizen of the United States of America." The delegates affirmed that "in order to claim our rights and fulfill our duties it is necessary for us to assimilate all we can that is best in the new civilization amidst which we shall have to live."

Forty years later, in Denver, Rodolfo (Corky) Gonzales, noted ex-featherweight and founder of the Crusade for Justice, declared, "We don't want to live in the world of the gringo, where people live in identical houses, mow their lawns at the same time, and compete with each other from dawn to dusk."

What has happened to bring about this change of attitude? LULAC is still going strong, especially in Texas, but now sponsors an aggressive program of educational reform and community action in the barrios. Even so, it is moderate alongside the militant Chicano groups that have mushroomed in the 1960s and '70s.

When did this new Chicano movement start? What touched off the young generation's outcry of *";Ya basta!"* (We're fed up!)?

Texas Mexicans might date the change from *La Marcha* of 1966, when 1,500 field workers walked under a summer sun from Rio Grande City to the capital at Austin, protesting wages as low as forty cents an hour. Or from the 1969 rally and manifesto following upon the governor's closing of a VISTA (Volunteers in Service to America) program in Del Rio. Or when La Raza Unida, led by José Angel Gutierrez, won control of the Crystal City school board and city council in 1970–71.

The watershed in New Mexico's Rio Arriba is the Tijerina land grant confrontation of 1967. A national milestone is the walkout of fifty Chicano delegates from a federal Equal Employment Commission Conference in Albuquerque in 1966. No Chicano sat on the Commission at the time, and the delegates complained that they were being talked down to. There was similar resentment the following year when a White House Conference on Mexican American Affairs failed to materialize. In its place there were hearings in El Paso. Calling this a meaningless gesture, Chicano activists organized a rival meeting in a South El Paso slum to discuss "gut issues."

The next year a Ford Foundation grant of $630,000 financed the establishment of a Southwest Council of La Raza,

with headquarters in Phoenix, for the "development of the
barrio through the organization and encouragement of local
cooperative community groups."

By this time, barrio papers like *La Raza* and *Inside Eastside*
of Los Angeles were popularizing the term "Chicano." A
Loyola University student conference stimulated campus
movements that were to coalesce in MECHA (Movimiento
Estudiantil Chicano de Aztlán). The name "Aztlán" and the
mystique surrounding it found wide acceptance after a National Youth Conference in Denver in 1969, sponsored by
Corky Gonzales and the Crusade for Justice. Out of it came
El Plan Espiritual de Aztlán (The Spiritual Plan of Aztlán),
affirming that "love for our brothers makes us a people whose
time has come." The Plan goes on to declare, "Before the
world, before all North America, before all our brothers in
the bronze continent, we are a nation. We are a union of free
pueblos. We are Aztlán."

The National Chicano Moratorium in East Los Angeles removed any lingering doubts concerning the reality of the nation's No. 2 minority problem. It was held on August 29,
1970, to protest the seemingly endless war in Vietnam, with
its exceptionally high Chicano combat casualties. Twenty
thousand marchers gathered in Laguna Park. Their intentions
were peaceful, to judge by the presence of women, children,
and babies in strollers. Picnic lunches were spread on the
grass. People were listening to a folk-singing group when
they heard the wail of police sirens, and then sheriff's deputies came bursting in, swinging clubs and firing tear gas

canisters. In the confusion, children were lost and fathers who went looking for them had run-ins with the white-helmeted deputies and were dragged into police cars.

Rioting now broke out and spread along Whittier Boulevard. In the course of a hot afternoon, windows were smashed and stores set on fire. The city police were called in. Casualties mounted. The nation's No. 1 Chicano journalist, Ruben Salazar, KMEX-TV news editor and *Los Angeles Times* columnist, was covering the story. He paused at the Silver Dollar Cafe and was sitting at the counter when a ten-inch tear gas projectile intended for siege operations was fired through the curtained doorway and crashed into his skull. He fell from his stool dead.

Depending on the individual, the Chicano movement may have begun with any of these events. Were Mexican Americans to be polled, probably a majority would date it from September 16, 1965, Mexican Independence Day, when *La Huelga,* the grape strike, was declared in Delano, California. A rural, not an urban happening, it nonetheless became a rallying point for farm workers, city workers, students, politicians, activists, clergymen, and sympathizing consumers of all ethnic groups. It was a training ground for future leaders, saw the birth of the Chicano theater, and demonstrated after more than fifty heartbreaking years that it really was possible to organize farm workers and hold them together in a union for collective bargaining. And it brought to national prominence Cesar Chavez, the best-loved Chicano leader of this generation.

Not all Chicanos are in perfect accord with Chavez. When tough young *vatos* are sprayed with pesticides on the picket line and all but run down on purpose by speeding pickup trucks, they find Cesar's counsels of nonviolence hard to take. Then there are the fasts and penances to which he is given: true, they tap the wellsprings of emotion in many of his people but they seem a waste of energy to those who have strayed from the flock or never been of it. No matter, everyone loves and honors Cesar Chavez, the Chicano counterpart of Martin Luther King, Jr.

Cesar was born into a large farm family near Yuma, Arizona, in 1927. His mother never turned away a hungry wanderer, white, brown, or black—and there were many of them passing through Yuma on the way to California as the Great Depression came on. The Chavez family, too, finally lost their farm in a tax sale and joined the sad procession, moving from crop to crop and sleeping under bridges when work was slack. Even with money in hand it wasn't easy to buy a hamburger sandwich, for restaurants displayed "White Trade Only" signs, meaning "Mexicans Keep Out."

After a World War II stint in the Navy, Chavez organized out of San Jose for the Community Service Organization and became its state director. In 1962 he left to devote himself to that most neglected group, the farm workers, who were denied protection under the national labor relations laws and left to the mercies of growers and labor contractors. Chavez didn't "talk union" to the workers at first. Memories of hardships endured and strikes broken ran too deep. What mat-

tered most was a credit union, to help them tide over between crops, and a cooperative gas station to provide cheaper
fuel for their trucks and jalopies as they moved north with
the ripening grapes.

While most grape pickers are Chicanos or Mexican nationals, there are also Blacks, Arabs, Asians, and poor Anglos. Chavez cautions his Raza brothers against racism, including anti-gringo cracks, saying, "Our belief is to help
everyone, not just one race. Humanity is our belief."

Early in September, 1965, the Filipino grape pickers at
Delano struck and sought Chavez's support. They were aging
men, drawn to California in the 1920s by the lure of a quick
stake but never earning enough to pay their passage home.
Chavez wasn't sure his group was ready to take on the
growers in a long, hard struggle, but they couldn't let the
Filipinos down. So on September 16 the Chicano pickers met
in a church hall under a portrait of Zapata and a red, white,
and black Aztec eagle flag and shouted for *La Huelga.*

The growers had political power, a half century's strike-
breaking experience, and a limitless supply of green-carders
and illegals no farther away than the border. It was up to the
pickets to tell the imported workers that a strike was on and
persuade them to leave the fields. Though like all Spanish-
speakers, the Chavez men had a torrent of abuse at their command, they often found it more effective to call out,
"Vénganse, señores, para su respeto y dignidad" (Come away,
gentlemen, as a matter of respect and dignity). But communication was not easy in the face of intimidation and ar-

rests. Nevertheless, other unions sent money, Senate subcommittee hearings were held, and California's Catholic bishops spoke out for a minimum wage and collective bargaining rights for farm workers.

In the Lenten season of 1966, Chavez led the strikers on a 300-mile pilgrimage to lay their cause before the governor. At their head was the banner of the Virgin of Guadalupe because, said a manifesto, "she is ours, all ours, patroness of the Mexican people. We also carry the Sacred Cross and the Star of David because we are not sectarians, and because we ask the help and prayers of all religions."

In every town along the San Joaquin Valley, where "the Mexican race has sacrificed itself for the last hundred years," the Chicano residents supplied food, shelter, and hospitality, heard the message, and saw the little plays that Luis Valdez had improvised for union meetings, taking off the *patroncito* (boss) and the *esquirol* (strikebreaker). The pilgrimage reached Sacramento on Easter Sunday. The governor had gone to Palm Springs to be with Frank Sinatra, but the United Farm Workers was able to announce that its first big contract had just been signed.

Other growers held out, and the strike had years to go. Picketing became increasingly dangerous and, as 1968 began, a year of world-wide unrest, there was increasing talk of meeting violence with violence. Chavez quietly undertook a Lenten fast as a prayer for peace and nonviolence. He continued for twenty-five days and, not a large man, lost thirty-five pounds. Every night a Franciscan priest offered a mass at the Forty Acres, the farm workers' headquarters. Pilgrims came from all over California to place candles before the altar and pin religious pictures to the union flag. Some slept in pup tents on the grounds to be near their saintly leader. ("I'm no saint," Chavez insists. "Ask my wife.") Robert F. Kennedy, the late President's brother, was with Cesar as the fast ended and broke bread with him.

Cesar Chavez, in his denim slacks and old sweater, is a soft-spoken man whose patent sincerity wins the hearts of men and women. From Berkeley and Los Angeles came motorcades bearing strike relief. Bearded students picketed the vineyards with priests and nuns, ministers and rabbis.

Pickets could be dispersed, but no one had to eat grapes. So a nationwide movement began to boycott table grapes. Strikers were dispatched to eastern cities to speak before unions and church societies, interview supermarket managers, and set up boycott committees and picket lines. La Huelga, La Causa, the Grape Boycott became a bond between the Chicanos and millions of Americans who cared.

The big break came in June, 1970, in the Coachella fields where the grapes ripen early and the growers began asking for "the Bird," meaning the right to put the union's Aztec eagle on their boxes. In July the Delano growers signed a similar agreement, providing an hourly rate, a piecework premium, pesticide controls, and a union hiring hall to stop labor contractor abuses.

So farm workers could be organized after all! Chavez had proved it. The lesson was not lost in other quarters. Lettuce

growers, seeing union handwriting on the wall, ducked the
Chavez organization by writing their field workers into a contract with the Anglo-dominated Teamsters Union. Many
grape growers followed suit in 1973 and 1974. "We shook
the tree," said Chavez, "and now the Teamsters are stealing
the fruit." To him it was another chapter in a tenacious
struggle that began in 1965 and might go on for many years,
requiring a mix of effective organizing efforts and consumer
boycott support.

Meanwhile the United Farm Workers has raised living
standards among farm workers and created an impressive list
of services for its members: medical clinics, a broad health
plan, social services, training programs, a credit union, coop-
eratives, and last but not least, an attractive retirement village at Delano. Named Agbayani Village for a Filipino
member who had died on the picket line, it was opened in
the summer of 1974 to its first residents, most of them Filipinos, too old now for the fields but union brothers to the
end.

 CHAPTER 25

THE SPIRIT
SPEAKS THROUGH
MY PEOPLE

O<small>F</small> the three faces, two are in profile: on the left, a bearded Spaniard; on the right, an Indian woman. In the center, full face, is their son, a Chicano youth, partaking of the features of both. This amulet, worn on a leather thong, bears the inscription: *Por mi raza habla el espíritu* (The spirit speaks through my people). It's the motto José Vasconcelos bestowed half a century ago on the National University of Mexico—only he used the future tense: *hablará* (will speak).

Vasconcelos, the minister of education who let the great muralists—Rivera, Orozco, Siqueiros—paint the walls of Mexico's public buildings, dreamed in those days of a cosmic race, *la raza cósmica,* built upon Christian love. A fifth race, ultimately embracing all others, it would flower first among Latin Americans, for whom feeling is a gateway to truth no less important than intellect. Vasconcelos likened their response to beauty to a burning bush or a heart in flame and considered it a happy complement to the technological genius of the United States.

As La Raza, Chicanos are in spiritual communion with their brothers and sisters in the lands below the Rio Grande. Some among them—Cesar Chavez, for example—are concerned that zeal for La Raza should not stand in the way of the larger goal of universal humanism. The younger militants reply that there can be no cosmic race until the Anglo "comes down off his high horse" and that meanwhile pride in La Raza and its values is not only justified but essential for survival. *¡Viva nuestra linda* (our beautiful) *Raza!* is the closing phrase of many letters to the Chicano press. Corky Gonzales tells his Crusaders for Justice, "Young leaders, teach your people to be proud of their names, their values, and their culture."

"Hunger brings me down, but pride lifts me up" (*El hambre me tumba y el orgullo me levanta*) runs a Chicano saying. It echoes Zapata's "Better die on your feet than live on your knees" (*Más vale morir parado que vivir de rodillas*) and the refrain of "La Valentina"—"If they are going to kill me tomorrow, let them kill me right away" (*Si me van a matar mañana, que me maten de una vez*).

Few Anglos realize the importance of pride to a people who have been so often humiliated in their dignity. But let no one imagine they lack humor. Theirs has a bite all its own that goes by the name of *vacilar*. Based on the contradictions between aspirations and painful reality, it is often compressed into proverbs. Work ennobles you, they say, but also ages you (*El trabajo te ennoblece, pero también te envejece*). When many dogs bark, only the first knows why (*Entre los perros que ladran, tan sólo el primero sabe porque lo hace*). Don't make me laugh, I'm shy a tooth (*No me hagan reir, que me falta un diente*). Always be skeptical; if Aristotle said an ox flew, it may be true, or it may not (*Aristóteles dijo que un buey voló, como puede ser que sí, puede ser que no*).

A polite storekeeper posts a sign in English or Spanish, asking his customers to spare him the embarrassment of denying them credit (*Evíteme la pena de negarle si pide fiado*). A caller is invited to take pot luck, or "lick a finger with us" (*que se chupe el dedo con nosotros*). "A family is judged by its manners," children are told. "Show respect and do not bring shame to our name."

If it is more blessed to give then to receive, it is also more delicate. A gift of money, clothing, or food, even to a close friend, implies that you are better off than the recipient and is a blow to his pride unless made with tact and proper excuses. It is best done when there can be an exchange of favors. "We are a communal people in the spirit of our Indian ancestors," says one Chicano. Children learn early to help care for their younger brothers and sisters. Home is a place of warmth and security.

Nothing so offends Chicanos as to be told they are "culturally deprived." That they are economically deprived no one knows better than those who suffer discrimination in their own flesh (*en su propia carne*). But culture is something else. Chicanos like their family loyalties, barrio associations, foods, songs, art, and language (though many wish they knew it better). Hard-working, they resent being typed as lazy by people who never chopped cotton for even half a day under the Imperial Valley sun.

Chicanos suffer from many stereotypes. The repertoire of the Chicano theater includes a piece in which a "typical Mexican" is offered for sale in four models: peasant asleep under big hat, knife-wielding drug pusher, revolutionist programmed to shout "Viva Villa!," and self-conscious *agringado*, Americanized in everything but complexion. The point is that Chicanos don't fit into a few simple types. They came from various regions and backgrounds, with diverse skills, beliefs, and levels of education, over a long period of time. Far from being passive and fatalistic, as often alleged, they settled the Southwest and were its pioneer ranchers and miners, as later they were the core of its labor force, numbered among its charter trade union members. Educators, in various studies, have found that a high proportion of Chicano pupils aspire to attend college and qualify for good jobs. In spite of this, reasons like "low aspirations" and "living for today" are still given to explain why Chicanos drop out of school and hold low-paying jobs. It's no longer fashionable to attribute such problems to race. But if the blame can be put on their culture, then all Chicanos can do is to hurry up and become like Anglos.

This the Chicanos are not likely to do. "He who disowns his people no longer has a mother" (*El que niega su raza ni madre tiene*), they say. He is a coconut, brown outside, white inside. Or a Malinche, like the Aztec maiden who abandoned her people to take up with Cortés. A Chicano paper used to carry a sketch of the "Malinche of the Month"—and to be nominated was no honor!

Juan used to become John on the first day of school, and in some places he still does. Why? Is Mary Helen a better name than Maria Elena? And what is wrong with Jesús, which Anglos nervously seek to change to Jesse? Jesús Ascension Arreola, Jr., likes his name as it is and wrote a poem to that effect entitled "My Name is Jesús."

Chicano critics find Anglo culture "bland" for their taste or "dehumanized and consumer-oriented." Not that they don't borrow from it. But they want to be free to pick and choose; they don't want "assimilation." Toward Black culture their feelings are mixed. Some rivalry exists over low-paying jobs for which the two groups compete, as it does over odds and ends of political patronage. But the Chicano movement owes much to the Black example, and many of its leaders recognize that both minorities will be stronger if they work together on common goals.

Perhaps Chicanos feel closest to the Indians, who are coming to call themselves Native Americans. The two minorities have little reason for rivalry, unless locally in New Mexico, and Chicanos are becoming more conscious of their Indian heritage. D-Q University at Davis, California, is a shared endeavor of Indians and Chicanos and "an assertion of the ability of the indigenous people to govern themselves." Named for Deganawidah, the Iroquois prophet, and the Mexican cul-

ture hero Quetzalcóatl, it espouses a life style that will pre-
serve the earth and its resources, including people.

One question keeps looming large. How are Chicanos to
relate to their blood brothers, variously known as wetbacks,
illegals, and Mexicans without documents? They are an inexhaustible source of cheap labor and often serve unintentionally as strikebreakers. In any case, they dare not complain
about wages and conditions. Cesar Chavez has stated his position: "We ask that any workers wishing to come from another country be allowed to come as free men, to immigrate
with their families and to organize here as they wish to."

At present, would-be immigrants are far more numerous
than those who may legally enter. The President of Mexico
has said, "We know that this problem will only be fully
resolved through our economic evolution when none of our
countrymen have to cross the frontier for lack of a means of
living here."

Meanwhile, *coyotes* (labor contractors and smugglers) are
bringing in illegals for $200 and $300 a head. Bert Corona,
an old-time labor organizer, estimates that around Los
Angeles alone there are half a million people without papers,
including a majority of those working in laundries, elec-
tronics plants, and the garment trades. Unlike other leaders,
he does not think the problem can be solved by roundups and
deportations that pit brother against brother, even son
against father. Believing that La Raza must stick together,
Corona is sponsoring an organization to defend people without documents by legal and political means.

All this is a troublesome issue, on which the Chicanos themselves are divided. One thing is sure. The problem will remain as long as there is work in the United States and people in Mexico through whom the stomach speaks.

Nonetheless the spirit speaks through them too. Not Vasconcelos but a later Mexican minister of education, Jaime Torres Bodet, staked out the claims of the imagination, even in times of distress, by comparing the cases of Robinson Crusoe and Sinbad the Sailor in the newspaper *Novedades*. Crusoe, like a good Anglo, turned his island paradise into a real estate development for nonexistent tourists. One searches his pages in vain for a description of a full moon or a tropical evening. Everything produces. Goats produce milk, grain produces bread, muskets produce wounds. The voice of a parrot summons Crusoe to work. He is not a wanderer but a colonist, governed by a passion to make his possessions secure. And so the discovery of a footprint on the beach fails to raise in him the hope of rescue but only makes him fear for his property.

On the other hand, when Sinbad the Sailor goes on perilous voyages, the hope of gain is merely a pretext for indulging his eternal curiosity. Each homecoming is a point of departure for another adventure. Even his fantastic landscapes are more authentic than Crusoe's. At least for Sinbad there are serpents that devour themselves and birds that do not talk!

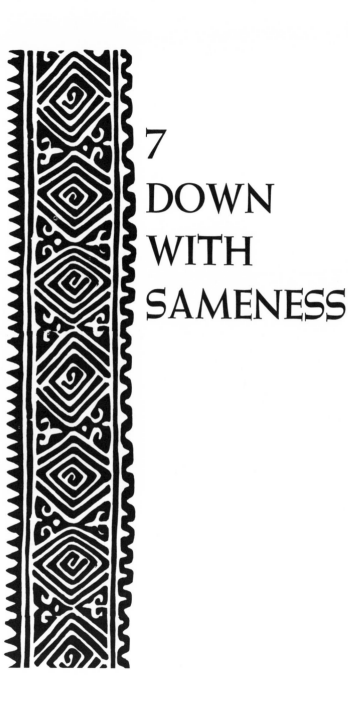

7
DOWN
WITH
SAMENESS

CHAPTER 26

TWO LANGUAGES
OR GO HUNGRY

CHICANOS who make their living among Anglos tell a cat-and-mouse joke. Whenever the mouse left its hole looking for food it ran a big risk and one day scurried to safety by only a whisker's breadth. From the security of its hide-out, the mouse heard a petulant *"Miáu, miáu."* That is how cats express chagrin in Spanish. The mouse was very still, and presently the yowling stopped. In its place there was a gruff *"Guáu, guáu,"* which means "bowwow." "Ah," thought the mouse, "the dog has chased the cat away and I can go out again." Alas, the little creature was no sooner in the open than the cat grabbed it. As she ate the tender morsel, she was heard to remark, "In this world anyone who doesn't speak two languages dies of hunger."

Pedro, like every Chicano whose mother tongue is Spanish, knows the cat is right. Only, as he looks back to his first day at school, long ago, he wonders if barking isn't easier than English. Pedro's name would have been changed to Peter ex-

179

cept for a classmate named Pete. Having two Peters in the same room would have been confusing.

Pete's Anglo father was in the export business. The family was just back from a year in Japan, and Pete was enrolled in the first grade. If his parents had stayed in Japan, he doubtless would be attending the American School in Tokyo. But suppose there was no American School? Pete at that moment might be sitting in a Japanese classroom. His situation, in that case, would be like Pedro's. He wouldn't know what the teacher was saying or how to answer her questions. If he stammered out something in English, would she say, "You are in Japan now, talk Japanese"?

Pete, like many six-year-olds, was imaginative. He imagined himself over there picking up Japanese expressions and a few written characters. When he forgot and spoke English and had to stay after school, he knew how to write "I will not speak English." The teacher had him write it a hundred times.

In his daydream, Pete memorized and wrote simple phrases without knowing what they meant, and read them too, though with a funny accent so that it was all the teacher could do to keep the other children from laughing. Numbers seemed harder. How could you follow the teacher's explanations without knowing the language? No wonder Pete wasn't ready at the end of the school year to go on to the second grade. He imagined himself spending two or three years with the beginners. By then he'd be so big they'd promote him anyway. His Japanese might improve but it wouldn't keep pace with the ever more difficult classwork. He knew that after a few discouraging years he would drop out of school.

What Pete merely imagined, Pedro experienced. Middle-aged now, he'd been taught by the old-fashioned sink-or-swim method, which held that Spanish-speaking pupils mustn't hear or speak a word of their native language or they'd never learn English. What English Pedro knows came at a high cost. In the first reader he became slightly acquainted with fair-haired Dick and Jane and their dog Spot, who was also white, but he couldn't keep abreast in reading ability and soon fell behind in arithmetic and geography. Without ever learning English well, he half forgot his Spanish. He felt ashamed of his "backward" family and even more of himself—and of course never made it to high school.

Pedro was not alone. In his time, half to three-quarters of the Spanish surnames dropped out of school—as many still do. Some knew, or picked up, enough English to complete the elementary grades before their lack of basic skills caught up with them. Scoring low on intelligence tests, they were often put into classes of "slow learners." It was not as widely recognized as it is today that one's I.Q. is bound to be low if he's unfamiliar with the language in which it is given and the culture with which it deals. Though every Anglo child knows what a jack-o'-lantern is, a Chicanito is more familiar with a *calavera,* a sugar-candy skull that is eaten on the Day of the Dead. Little Red Riding Hood is *Caperucita Roja,* but who from south of the Rio Grande ever heard of Mother Goose?

The late George I. Sanchez, a University of Texas educator, once tested a group of Chicanos in the second grade. They averaged 72. After two years of remedial instruction they were retested and had climbed to 100.

In Pedro's time, not many Chicanos persevered through high school. Fewer still went to college and, if they did, English became their dominant language, and everyone said what a pity a student named Padilla or Ramirez knew so little Spanish.

In recent years, educators have discovered better ways of teaching English. Listening comes first, along with speaking simple sentences. Reading and writing are learned in the pupil's native Spanish. Gradually, after English becomes understandable, these reading and writing skills are transferred to the new language. When this method is used, Chicanos are taught in Spanish until they can follow the teacher in English. then the work is given partly in Spanish, partly in English. As the second language is learned, the mother tongue, in which the deepest human emotions are rooted, is being strengthened.

This is bilingual education, which the United States Office of Education defines as "the use of two languages, one of which is English, as mediums of instruction for the same pupil population in a well-organized program which encompasses part or all of the curriculum and includes the study of the history and culture associated with the mother tongue. A complete program develops and maintains the children's self-esteem and a legitimate pride in both cultures."

An Office of Education report on seventy-eight bilingual

education projects launched in 1969 concludes that the children make better progress in school, become more proficient both in English and in their mother tongue, and develop an understanding and respect for the culture associated with the mother tongue that lead to a more positive self-image and better social and personal adjustment.

Bilingual education in this broad sense is also bicultural education. It is more than remedial reading and ESL (English as a second language) programs, which teach "survival English" for an hour or two a day. Bicultural education builds on two languages and helps pupils become aware of themselves as products of the culture of Mexico and the United States. Rather than turning children against the ways of their parents, it strengthens the ties between school and home.

To date, bicultural education is more of a demonstration of what can be done than a widespread reality. Its beginnings have been financed by federal funds voted by Congress. Most of the first programs were set up in districts with a Chicano majority and an Anglo and Black minority. While Chicanos learn English, the others learn Spanish. In a well-run program, everyone becomes fluently bilingual by the fifth or sixth grade. A good command of Spanish is of practical value in the Southwest, especially near the border, while the widening of cultural horizons that comes with knowing more of Mexico and the Indian past is to many a welcome if unexpected bonus. Ideally, bicultural education would continue to high school and beyond, enriching the regional culture.

Bilingualism also gives much-needed recognition to the

Mexican American child. Formerly he was on the receiving end, learning English. Now he has something to give—his language and culture—that the Anglo child wants to learn about. It does wonders for the Chicano's self-image, reports a Laredo, Texas, school official.

An Albuquerque educator finds that pupils who are encouraged to take pride in their native Spanish also become more proficient in English. The Albuquerque program calls for teaching social studies, for example, in Spanish, math in English, and language and reading in both. Pomona, California, teaches math in Spanish, as well as geography and world history. Most subjects can be taught in either language. However, Mexican literature goes better in Spanish and spelling in English. Spelling is less of a problem in Spanish, for words are written more nearly as they are pronounced. Pueblo, Colorado, besides teaching English to Hispanos and Spanish to Anglos, reinforces the Spanish of children who have half-forgotten their parents' language.

Like other cities with bicultural programs, El Paso features the folklore, songs, dances, poetry, holidays, and national heroes of both the United States and Mexico. Critics have pointed out the importance of presenting the early Southwest as it really was, burying once and for all the "fantasy heritage" that limits the cast of characters to kindly padres, Spanish caballeros, and señoritas with gardenias behind their ears, with some shiftless Indians and Mexicans thrown in for atmosphere.

The recent surge of interest in bicultural education found

the United States with no more than an estimated 2,000 qualified bicultural teachers. Few Anglo teachers were fluent enough in Spanish to teach in that language without additional preparation. And too few Chicanos had received teacher training at all. Colleges and universities in the Southwest now offer bilingual-bicultural studies to prospective teachers, but meanwhile it has been necessary to train working teachers for new responsibilities. At institutes and summer training workshops they improve their Spanish and become sensitized to the nation's Indo-Hispanic background. Sometimes two teachers operate as a team, one in English, the other in Spanish. Each teaches a group in the morning, then moves to the other group in the afternoon. Bilingual aides are recruited among housewives and high school and college students. They lend the teacher a hand with games and rest periods and even help with instruction. Bilingual programs may begin as early as kindergarten or even before.

A successful bicultural program needs the support of an advisory council of community leaders. Parents are encouraged to take an interest in their children's schoolwork. Some serve as volunteers and demonstrate the crafts, dances, music, and foods that are typical of their culture. Audio-visual materials are in demand: filmstrips, animated color films, teaching machines, and audiotapes to which pupils may listen while their teacher is busy with another group. The talents of writers, musicians, artists, and actors are all utilized in preparing materials to explain and enrich bicultural education.

"Down with sameness" is one of the slogans that Chicanos have painted on barrio walls. The existing bicultural programs are only a hint of what is possible when adequate funds, talent, and popular support are mobilized. The United States is too big for everyone to be alike and is better off for some interesting variety.

CHAPTER 27

CHICANO RENAISSANCE

THE Aztecs' *xochitl in cuicatl* translates as *flor y canto,* flower and song. It means poetry and more. *Floricanto en Aztlán* is a collection of Alurista's poems, published at the University of California in Los Angeles. Alurista is Alberto Baltazar Urista Heredia, San Diego High School, '65. He went on to study and teach at San Diego State College. Imbued with the barrios' rhythms and feeling tone, he moves effortlessly between English and Spanish or reaches into the Mesoamerican past. Speaking of his people, Alurista says we've played cowboys as opposed to Indians, forgetting that the ancestors of our charro grandfathers were themselves Indians.

Alurista is also director of Servidores del Arbol de la Vida (Servants of the Tree of Life), a theater group which is also a dance group and a musical ensemble. No need to draw sharp lines between the arts. A poem may be read, but why not sing it, dance to it, accompany it with the flute and guitar or with congas and bongos?

Canto y grito mi liberación (*I Sing and Shout My Liberation*) is Ricardo Sanchez's title for a collection of his poems. *"Canto mi épica Chicana"* (I sing my Chicano epic), announces Sergio Elizondo in *Perros y antiperros,* a poetic sequence touching the years since the coming of blue-eyed strangers who were hospitably received, then proceeded to take over the land.

Omar Salinas, "the crazy gypsy," celebrates his mother's beauty and asserts the dignity of his Aztec line. In *I Am Joaquín,* Corky Gonzales is all Chicanos and their forebears: Cuauhtémoc and Cortés, Hidalgo and Juárez, the despots Díaz and Huerta, and the liberators Madero and Zapata. He rides with Pancho Villa and is in the eyes of a black-shawled woman.

Scores of poets have blossomed in the Chicano renaissance since the mid-1960s. They show up everywhere—in the barrios, the colleges, the prisons.

The Southwest also bears witness to an art renaissance. Los Toltecas de Aztlán, a San Diego artists' group, exhibits regularly in schoolhouses and barrio halls. Chicano themes embellish the walls of the Aztec Center at San Diego State College. In Los Angeles, Chicano canvases hang in fashionable galleries on La Cienega Boulevard, while on Eastside walls and fences amateurs and professionals make rain gods and plumed serpents come alive in bright primitive colors. La Casa de la Raza in Santa Barbara has some noted murals, while San Francisco's Mission District flaunts people's art on the sides of schools and youth centers. The neighborhood legal aid building bears pictures of police and courtroom abuses. Another wall shows wasting addicts injecting heroin and slipping into some Aztec realm of the dead.

The Chicano theater, stemming from the grape strike, numbers scores of groups, now federated in a Teatro Nacional de Aztlán. It is not commercial theater, uses few props, dispenses with scenery, and needs only a meeting hall, a flatbed truck, or a vacant lot for a stage. The little plays, or *actos,* run ten or fifteen minutes and are often enlivened by song, music, and dancing. "Don't say it, do it" is a Chicano motto, having in mind that a good acto takes the place of many speeches. Chicano theater is education, affirmation, and social satire, seasoned with inimitable folk humor. The actors are amateurs, often students, and the groups call themselves Teatro Mestizo, Grupo Quetzalcóatl, Los Topos (The Moles), Teatro de los Barrios, and the like. Las Cucarachas (The Cockroaches) is a San Francisco all-women's group.

Though Chicano theater aims to be bilingual, its young talent has been schooled more in English than Spanish. They came, thirty groups, to Mexico City in the summer of 1974 in their jeans, headbands, and embroidered skirts, for the fifth annual Chicano theater festival, joining for the first time with similar groups from Mexico and Central and South America. For two weeks the festival played to packed houses. The Chicanos bravely spoke their lines in Spanish as much as possible and received warm fraternal applause for either language.

The Chicano renaissance is a search for identity by a people who have been too much left out of United States history.

They are trying through education to find out who they are. Education takes various forms. In Chicago, the Loop College Center for Continuing Education offers a course on *Nuestra Comunidad* (Our Community) at Casa Aztlán. It deals with educational goals, community health, political awareness, and the Mexican cultural heritage and is an example of short courses for adults.

In Denver, the Crusade for Justice operates a year-round school from kindergarten through college. It bears the name of Tlatelolco for the Aztec school where the Chicanos' Indian forefathers demonstrated their high capacity for learning to their Franciscan teachers more than four centuries ago. Cooperation among pupils is fostered, for competitive learning is considered alien to Mexican culture. Besides basic subjects, the curriculum includes arts and crafts, writing-journalism, business courses, and an intensive study each year of one pre-Hispanic culture. College studies include community organization, Latin American affairs, and teaching experience with younger pupils. A folk-dancing troupe has studied with several Mexican institutes and tours as the Ballet Chicano de Aztlán.

In 1970 Chicanos were a seventh of California's population but came to less than a twentieth of the enrollment on most college campuses. Since then, Chicano studies programs have been pushed in this and other states, while student organizations and groups like the League of United Latin American Citizens are promoting enrollment. Applicants are likely to need not only loans and scholarships but an orientation to campus life, comradeship, tutoring and counseling, and perhaps a redirection of personal goals. Two-year community colleges and the lower divisions of four-year institutions provide an introduction to Chicano studies, along with training in written and oral expression in English and Spanish. Upper-division students concentrate on specialized courses in the humanities, the social sciences, or education. Four-year programs lead to a bachelor's degree, and for some are a stepping stone to professional training in medicine, law, and teaching, where qualified Chicanos are particularly needed.

Chicano studies programs are regarded not as a means by which students may raise themselves out of the barrios but as a preparation for effective service to the barrios. Student organizations encourage members to be active in community affairs as an essential part of their education. To maintain close ties between campus and barrio, Chicano leaders recommend that Chicano studies program governing boards be nominated by Chicanos and represent students, faculty, administrators, employees, and other members of the Chicano community.

Chicano students feel drawn to Mexico as a mother country (Spain being more of a grandparent). Mexico has experienced remarkable development since the revolutions and civil wars of two generations ago. Some of its rich literature is available in English translation for those not yet at home in literary Spanish. *Pedro Páramo,* a favorite in Mexican literature courses, is Juan Rulfo's haunting story of a young man searching for his father. Some consider it the great Mexican novel; others give that place to *Al filo del agua (On the Edge of the*

Storm), in which Agustín Yáñez records the first tremors of the 1910 Revolution as they were felt in a Jalisco village. Carlos Fuentes has fans in several languages. Chicanos are apt to make his acquaintance through *La muerte de Artemio Cruz* (*The Death of Artemio Cruz*), the reveries of an expiring man who gave up revolutionary principles for power.

Besides much else from Mexico, there's all of Latin America, including Jorge Luis Borges and Julio Cortázar, Argentine masters of the short story; the poems of the late Pablo Neruda of Chile, including bilingual editions; and the Colombian Gabriel García Márquez's *Cien años de soledad* (*One Hundred Years of Solitude*), the humor, pathos, and "magic realism" of which have captured the imagination of a continent.

Surprisingly often, teachers in Chicano studies programs are themselves storytellers of note, playing a dual role in the Chicano renaissance. Tomas Rivera, a Texas professor, wrote *". . . y no se lo tragó la tierra,"* which is published with an accompanying translation. It follows a Chicano child's emotional growth over a crucial year, telling how he ceases feeling helpless before fate, and yet the earth does not part! Rodolfo A. Anaya, an Albuquerque schoolteacher, wrote *Bless Me, Ultima* in English. It is another story of a boy's growing up, aided in this case by the sensitive insight of a practitioner of traditional folk medicine.

These and other Chicano books, as well as the quarterly journal *El Grito,* are published by Quinto Sol Publications of Berkeley, whose co-editor, Octavio I. Romano-V., is a Uni-

versity of California anthropologist. From the Chicano Studies Center at the University of California in Los Angeles
comes another quarterly, *Aztlán—A Chicano Journal of the
Social Sciences and the Arts.* The Chicano renaissance is rich in
publications, though not all have the financial means for a
long life.

To appreciate the sense of identity that Chicanos have
acquired in recent years, it is enough to read novels like
these, or Richard Vasquez's *Chicano* and Raymond Barrio's
The Plum Plum Pickers, and then compare them with *Pocho,*
which José Antonio Villarreal published in 1959, when the
goal of Mexican Americans was assimilation into Anglo society. Richard, the protagonist, fails in his search for identity.
Unlike his father, he has no memory of the Mexican Revolution. At the same time, his efforts to be an American meet
with frustration. Finding no identity, he does without one
and joins the Army.

 CHAPTER 28

TWO CULTURES
BETTER THAN ONE

MILLIONS of Americans have had two years of French in high school or college and have later visited Europe on a package tour. The waiters in Paris, to their chagrin, couldn't understand them at all. They had to order by pointing to the menu! Some of them concluded that studying foreign languages is a waste of time and it would be better if everyone spoke English.

Europeans look at foreign languages in a different light. All the more so if they live in one of the smaller countries. A Netherlands businessman does business in English, French, German, and Dutch. Many a Swiss speaks his country's three major languages—German, French, Italian—and English besides. There's a bookstore in Helsinki with kilometers of shelved books in many languages. No well-read Finn dreams of limiting himself or herself to Finnish.

It's not unusual to meet a Scandinavian, newly arrived in the United States, whose English bears hardly a trace of an

accent. Some people try to explain such things by saying that
Europeans have a "talent" for languages and Americans don't.
But the fact is that Europeans don't expect to become fluent
in English after two years. That near-flawless accent is a
reward for eight, ten, or twelve years of study, beginning as
early as kindergarten. Few Americans feel that much need for
another language.

It is different in Canada, where French is the dominant
language in Quebec and a minority language in other provinces. Canada has accepted a goal of becoming bilingual in
English and French. Even the Queen bears greetings in
French when she visits Montreal.

Would the earth part if the President of the United States
saluted a San Antonio audience in Spanish? Be that as it may,
San Antonio, Los Angeles, and other Chicano strongholds are
sure to become increasingly bilingual. Chicanos, even as they
learn English better, will seek to repair the ravages to their
Spanish for the sake of their cultural identity. For, as they
say, "If the language goes, the culture goes."

Anglos in Spanish-speaking surroundings will come to feel
the same need for Spanish that a Dutch merchant has for English. An employer needing a Spanish-speaking staff will see
how foolish it was to make Chicano children stop talking
their native Spanish, only to teach some imperfect Spanish
later on to English-speaking adults.

Experience has amply shown that a second language comes
easily when begun early and learned as part of a living culture
rather than as a "Where is the pen of my aunt?" drill. It is

the culture that matters. The language is a key that opens
doors to a wonderful world of diversity. If it qualifies Chicanos for greater participation in the nation's life, it can free
Anglos from a one-language, one-culture prison in which
they have been unwittingly living.

In these times of weakening family ties, dwindling resources, and unforeseen environmental hazards, can we be sure
that one culture has all the answers? Can Anglos learn to respect if not imitate the Chicanos' less competitive ways of living together?

One thing is sure. The Southwest's Chicanos, some of
them expanding into the Northwest and the Midwest, will
not be content to remain just hewers of wood and drawers of
water. As they strive for a full share in the society to which
they belong, they will meet resistance in some quarters, acceptance in others. If the walls raised against them are too
high to scale, they will withdraw into hostile isolation and a
long period of conflict may ensue.

The alternative is cultural pluralism, which means that
each culture will have its respected place and every individual
will be free to choose the elements he may find attractive in
another life style. Understanding between the cultures will
depend more on mutual respect, however, than on elimina-
tion of differences. When the languages of Shakespeare and
Cervantes, and the cultures that go with them, are widely
known by Chicanos and Anglos alike, the American Southwest will come into a rich bicultural inheritance which other
regions may care one day to emulate after their own fashion.

CHICANO TALK

THE following expressions include examples of standard and provincial Spanish, youth argot, and semi-English *pochismos:*

agringado (ah-green-GAH-doh)—become like a gringo or Anglo
aquí sí, ése (ah-KEE SEE EHS-ey)—right here, guy
barrio—neighborhood, ward
bil de la luz (beel day lah loose)—light bill
bolilla (bo-LEE-yah)—Anglo girl
bracero—worker admitted by international agreement
Californio—Californian of Spanish-Mexican period
carnal (kahr-NAHL)—brother
carnalismo—brotherhood
charro—gentleman cattleman in dress riding habit
la chota—the police
cortito—short-handled hoe
coyote—fixer, labor smuggler
gabacho—gringo, Anglo
híjole! (EE-ho-lay)—wow!
Hispano (ees-PAH-no)—New Mexico Spanish American or of other Spanish-speaking background
la jefa (lah HAY-fah)—mother as household manager
Mexicano (may-he-CAH-no)—Mexican; of Mexican descent

la migra (lah ME-grah)—Border Patrol of Immigration Service

mojado (moh-HAH-doh)—wetback, one who enters country irregularly as by swimming Rio Grande

órale, carnal (OH-rah-lay kahr-NAHL)—say, brother; O.K.

patrón, patroncito—boss, employer

la pelona—figuratively, death. Also, *la calaca*

pinta—penitentiary

pinto—prisoner

pocho—Mexican with Anglo traits

ponte águila (PONE-tay AH-gee-lah)—watch out

que gacho!—how crummy!

La Raza (lah RAH-sah)—people of Mexican descent; more broadly, Latin Americans

rinche—Texas Ranger

ruca—girl, woman

simón, carnal! (see-MOHN kahr-NAHL)—right, man!

Tejano (tay-HAH-no)—Texas Mexican

Tío Taco—Uncle Taco, an Uncle Tom type

vato loco—crazy guy, street kid, dude. Also, *bato loco*

vendido (vane-DEE-do)—a sellout

wáchele, ése (WATCH-ey-lay EHS-ey)—watch it, you

ya basta!—fed up!

ya mero mano—almost, pal

FOR FURTHER READING

CHICANO ANTHOLOGIES

Castañeda Shular, Antonia; Ybarra-Frausto, Tomás; and Sommers, Joseph; eds. *Literatura Chicana: Texto y Contexto*. English and Spanish. Englewood Cliffs, N.J.: Prentice-Hall, 1972.

Ludwig, Ed, and Santibañez, James, eds. *The Chicanos: Mexican American Voices*. Baltimore: Penguin, 1971.

Nava, Julian, ed. *¡Viva la Raza! Readings on Mexican Americans*. New York: Van Nostrand, 1973.

Ortego, Philip D., ed. *We Are Chicanos: An Anthology of Mexican-American Literature*. New York: Washington Square Press, 1973.

Paredes, Américo, and Paredes, Raymund, eds. *Mexican American Authors*. Boston: Houghton Mifflin, 1972.

Romano-V., Octavio Ignacio, and Ríos C., Herminio, eds. *El Espejo—The Mirror: Selected Chicano Literature*. English and Spanish. rev. ed. Berkeley, Ca.: Quinto Sol, 1972.

Salinas, Luis Omar, and Faderman, Lillian, eds. *From the Barrio: A Chicano Anthology*. San Francisco: Canfield, 1973.

Valdez, Luis, and Steiner, Stan, eds. *Aztlan: An Anthology of Mexican American Literature*. New York: Vintage, 1972.

CHICANO LITERATURE AND ART

Alurista. *Floricanto en Aztlán.* Los Angeles: Chicano Cultural Center, University of California, 1971. Poems.

Anaya, Rudolfo A. *Bless Me, Ultima.* Berkeley, Ca.: Quinto Sol, 1972. Novel.

Delgado, Abelardo. *Chicano: 25 Pieces of a Chicano Mind.* Santa Barbara, Ca.: La Causa, 1971. Poems.

Elizondo, Sergio. *Perros y Antiperros: Una Epica Chicana.* Poem in Spanish with English translation. Berkeley, Ca.: Quinto Sol, 1972.

Gonzales, Rodolfo. *I Am Joaquín. Yo Soy Joaquín.* Poem in English and Spanish. New York: Bantam, 1972.

Hinojosa-S., Rolando R. *Estampas del Valle y Otras Obras. Sketches of the Valley and Other Works.* Spanish and English. Berkeley, Ca.: Quinto Sol, 1973.

Quirate, Jacinto. *Mexican American Artists.* Austin: University of Texas Press, 1973.

Rivera, Tomás. *"y no se lo tragó la tierra."* Spanish, with English translation, *"and the earth did not part."* Berkeley, Ca.: Quinto Sol, 1971.

Salinas, Omar. *Crazy Gypsy.* Fresno, Ca.: Origenes, 1971. Poems.

Sanchez, Ricardo. *Canto y Grito Mi Liberación.* Garden City, N.Y.: Anchor, 1973. Poems.

Vasquez, Richard. *Chicano.* New York: Avon, 1971. Novel.

Villarreal, José Antonio. *Pocho.* Garden City, N.Y.: Anchor, 1970. Novel.

CONTEMPORARY CHICANO SCENE

Burma, John H., ed. *Mexican-Americans in the United States: A Reader.* Cambridge, Ma.: Schenkman, 1970.

Carranza, Eliu. *Pensamientos on los Chicanos: A Cultural Revolution.* Berkeley: California Book, 1969.

De la Garza, Rudolph O.; Kruszewski, Z. Anthony; and Arciniega,

Tomás A.; eds. *Chicanos and Native Americans: The Territorial Minorities.* Englewood Cliffs, N.J.: Prentice-Hall, 1973.

Galarza, Ernesto. *Merchants of Labor: The Mexican Bracero Story.* Santa Barbara, Ca.: McNally & Loftin, 1964.

Galarza, Ernesto; Gallegos, Herman; and Samora, Julian. *Mexican-Americans in the Southwest.* Santa Barbara, Ca.: McNally & Loftin, 1969.

Gardner, Richard. *¡Grito! Reies Tijerina and the New Mexico Land Grant War of 1967.* New York: Harper Colophon, 1971.

Gomez, David F. *Somos Chicanos: Strangers in Our Own Land.* Boston: Beacon, 1973.

Grebler, Leo; Moore, Joan W.; and Guzman, Ralph C. with others. *The Mexican-American People. The Nation's Second Largest Minority.* New York: Free Press, 1970. Based on Mexican-American Study Project, University of California, Los Angeles.

Haddox, John. *Los Chicanos: An Awakening People.* El Paso: Texas Western Press, 1970.

Matthiessen, Peter. *Sal Si Puedes: Cesar Chavez and the New American Revolution.* New York: Dell, 1973.

Moore, Joan W., with Alfred Cuéllar. *Mexican Americans.* Englewood Cliffs, N.J.: Prentice-Hall, 1970.

Morales, Armando. *Ando Sangrando: A Study of Mexican American-Police Conflict.* La Puente, Ca.: Perspectiva, 1972.

Nelson, Eugene. *Huelga: The First Hundred Days of the Great Delano Grape Strike.* Delano, Ca.: Farm Worker Press, 1966.

Rendon, Armando B. *Chicano Manifesto.* New York: Collier, 1972.

Rivas, Gilberto L. *The Chicanos: Life and Struggles of the Mexican Minority in the United States, with Readings.* New York: Monthly Review, 1973.

Romano-V., Octavio Ignacio, ed. *Voices: Readings from El Grito.* rev. ed. Berkeley, Ca.: Quinto Sol, 1973.

Rubel, Arthur J. *Across the Tracks: Mexican-Americans in a Texas City.* Austin: University of Texas Press, 1971.

Steiner, Stan. *La Raza: The Mexican Americans*. New York: Harper Colophon, 1970.

United States Commission on Civil Rights. *Mexican Americans and the Administration of Justice in the Southwest*. Washington, D.C.: Government Printing Office, 1970.

CHICANOS AND HEALTH

Clark, Margaret. *Health in the Mexican-American Culture: A Community Study*. 2nd ed. Berkeley: University of California Press, 1970.

CHICANOS AND EDUCATION

Carter, Thomas P. *Mexican Americans in School: A History of Educational Neglect*. New York: College Entrance Examination Board, 1970.

Forbes, Jack D. *Mexican-Americans, A Handbook for Educators*. Washington, D.C.: Educational Systems, 1966.

Hernandez, Luis F. *A Forgotten American: A Resource Unit for Teachers on the Mexican American*. New York: Anti-Defamation League of B'nai B'rith, 1969.

Johnson, Henry Sioux, and Hernandez, William J., eds. *Educating the Mexican American*. Valley Forge, Pa.: Judson, 1970.

National Association of Elementary School Principals. The National Elementary Principal 50:2 (Nov. 1970), Washington, D.C. Issue devoted to education for the Spanish-speaking.

United States Commission on Civil Rights. *Mexican American Education Study. Report I: Ethnic Isolation of Mexican Americans in the Public Schools of the Southwest*. Washington, D.C.: Government Printing Office, 1971. Also *Report II: The Unfinished Education*, 1971. *Report III: The Excluded Student*, 1972. *Report IV: Mexican American Education in Texas: A Function of Wealth*, 1972. *Report V: Teachers and Students*, 1973.

SOUTHWESTERN BACKGROUND

Bishop, Morris. *The Odyssey of Cabeza de Vaca.* Westport, Conn.: Greenwood, 1971.

Bolton, Herbert Eugene. *The Padre on Horseback.* Introduction by John Francis Bannon, S.J. Chicago: Loyola University Press, 1963. Reprint of a study published in 1932.

Castillo, Pedro, and Camarillo, Albert, eds. *Furia y Muerte: Los Bandidos Chicanos.* In English. Los Angeles: Aztlán Publications, 1974. Chicano folk heroes.

Cortes, Carlos E., ed. *The Penitentes of New Mexico.* New York: Arno, 1974. Reprint of materials published in 1893, 1935, and 1937.

Crichton, Kyle S. *Law and Order, Ltd. The Rousing Life of Elfego Baca of New Mexico.* Glorieta, N.M.: Rio Grande Press, 1970. Reprint of edition published in 1928.

Folsom, Franklin. *Red Power on the Rio Grande: The Native American Revolution of 1680.* Chicago: Follett, 1973.

Galarza, Ernesto. *Barrio Boy.* Notre Dame, Ind.: University of Notre Dame Press, 1971. Autobiography.

Gamio, Manuel. *The Life Story of the Mexican Immigrant.* New York: Dover, 1971. Reprint of autobiographical documents published in 1931.

————. *Mexican Immigration to the United States.* New York: Dover, 1971. Reprint of study published in 1930.

McWilliams, Carey. *North from Mexico: The Spanish-Speaking People of the United States.* New York: Greenwood, 1968.

Meier, Matt S., and Rivera, Feliciano. *The Chicanos: A History of Mexican Americans.* New York: Hill and Wang, 1972.

Nava, Julian. *Mexican Americans: Past, Present, and Future.* New York: American Book, 1969.

Paredes, Américo. *"With His Pistol in His Hand." A Border Ballad and Its Hero.* Austin: University of Texas Press, 1971. Story of Gregorio Cortez.

Pitt, Leonard. *The Decline of the Californios*. Berkeley: University of California Press, 1971.

Robinson, Cecil. *With the Ears of Strangers: The Mexican in American Literature*. Tucson: University of Arizona Press, 1963.

Taylor, Paul S. *Mexican Labor in the United States*. 2 vols. New York: Arno, 1970. Reprints of studies published from 1928 to 1932.

MEXICAN AND PRE-HISPANIC BACKGROUND

Bernal, Ignacio. *Mexico Before Cortez: Art, History, Legend*. Garden City, N.Y.: Anchor, 1963.

Coe, Michael D. *America's First Civilization: Discovering the Olmec*. New York: American Heritage, 1968.

———. *Mexico*. New York: Praeger, 1962. Also *The Maya*, 1966. Mesoamerican cultures.

Coy, Harold. *Man Comes to America*. Boston: Little, Brown, 1973.

———. *The Mexicans*. Boston: Little, Brown, 1970.

Elting, Mary, and Folsom, Michael. *The Mysterious Grain: Science in Search of the Origin of Corn*. New York: M. Evans, 1967.

Leon-Portilla, Miguel. *Aztec Thought and Culture: A Study of the Ancient Nahuatl Mind*. Norman: University of Oklahoma Press, 1970.

———, ed. *The Broken Spears*. Boston: Beacon, 1969. The Spanish Conquest through Indian eyes.

———. *Pre-Columbian Literature of Mexico*. Norman: University of Oklahoma Press, 1969.

Peterson, Frederick A. *Ancient Mexico: An Introduction to the Pre-Hispanic Cultures*. New York: Capricorn, 1969.

Womack, John. *Zapata and the Mexican Revolution*. New York: Knopf, 1969.

LATIN AMERICAN AUTHORS

Belitt, Ben, ed. *Selected Poems of Pablo Neruda*. Spanish and English. New York: Evergreen, 1961.

Borges, Jorge L. *Aleph and Other Stories*. New York: Bantam, 1971. Also
    Doctor Brodie's Report, 1973.
Cortázar, Julio. *Blow-up and Other Stories*. New York: Collier, 1968.
Fuentes, Carlos. *The Death of Artemio Cruz*. New York: Farrar, Straus,
    1964. Novel.
García Márquez, Gabriel. *One Hundred Years of Solitude*. New York: Avon,
    1971. Novel.
Paz, Octavio, ed. *New Poetry of Mexico*. New York: Dutton, 1970.
Rulfo, Juan. *Pedro Páramo*. New York: Grove, 1959. Novel.
Yañez, Agustín. *The Edge of the Storm*. Austin: University of Texas Press,
    1963. Novel.

INDEX